COLORADO
GUNSMOKE

COLORADO GUNSMOKE

True Stories
of Outlaws
and Lawmen
on the
Colorado
Frontier

KEN JESSEN

J.V. Publications • Loveland, Colorado

First Edition
   3 4 5 6 7 8 9

Printed in the United States of America

Library of Congress Cataloging-in-Publication Data

Jessen, Kenneth Christian.
   Colorado gunsmoke.

   Bibliography: p.
   Includes index.
   1. Outlaws—Colorado.   2. Crime and criminals—
Colorado—History—19th century.   3. Colorado—
History.   4. Frontier and pioneer life—Colorado.
I. Title.
F776.J47   1986   978.8'03   86-3248
ISBN 0-9611662-5-8

Cover Design by LaVonne Kaseman

This book is dedicated to
Dave, Beth, Steven, Lanette, and Jessica Dahl

CONTENTS

ACKNOWLEDGMENTS

I would like to thank Lee Kline and Lee Gregory for being my first editors for *Colorado Gunsmoke*. They made many valuable contributions, allowing me to quickly get the final manuscript into good shape. Next, I would like to thank Pruett editor Merilee Eggleston for her work on improving the manuscript, and Susan Becker for her final copyediting.

Help in finding the right photographs came from Augie Mastrogiuseppe at the Denver Public Library's Western History Department (this is the fourth book we have worked on together) and Mercedes Penarowski at the Colorado Historical Society. In addition, John Lovett at the University of Oklahoma Library found several photographs not available in other collections.

Gwen Goldsberry, a professional researcher, was brought in to aid in the location of certain documents and newspaper articles. She did an excellent job of gathering supporting information.

Bill Reed's expertise was called upon in the area of black powder percussion revolvers.

A big debt of gratitude is owed to Roy O'Dell of Cambridge, England, for his supply of historical information on gunfights in Colorado. Roy also checked on many of the specific details in various stories. Distance has not hampered Roy's ability to save, file, and collect information on the American West.

Lorna Hammill did the clean-up work on the final manuscript, using her laser printer to produce the final draft.

And I must thank my wonderful wife, Sonje, for putting up with me while I produced this book.

Kenneth Jessen
Loveland, Colorado, 1986

INTRODUCTION

The late 1800s were exciting and formative years for Colorado. Beginning with the gold rush in 1859, the early settlers attracted to the state formed a volatile mixture of honest people and fortune seekers. Some had honorable intentions of prospecting, mining, ranching, freighting, farming, and merchandising. Others were out to separate the "greenhorns" from their cash in the gambling halls, saloons, and bordellos or simply by robbery. Typical of the American West, Colorado attracted some of the best and the worst.

These opposing elements of good and evil were the hallmarks of the exciting era covered in *Colorado Gunsmoke*, and they affected the style of justice in frontier towns. Lynchings were one quick way to deal with the lack of an efficient legal system. In some instances, murder was accepted by the people of Colorado as a way of settling differences. But the persistence of Colorado's law officers and detectives in their pursuit of criminals finally brought law and order to the region.

Another aspect of *Colorado Gunsmoke* is the amazing variety of crimes committed before the turn of the century. Some crimes were the result of mob rule, some the result of greed, and others were acts of spontaneous violence. A clear motive was not always apparent.

These stories are meant not only to inform, but to entertain.

A WORD ABOUT THE RESEARCH

Unfortunately, many of the stories about the gunfights that took place in early Colorado have been exaggerated over the years. Embellishment upon the actual facts always makes for better reading. Even the reporters of that time took advantage of their opportunities to make certain events bigger than life.

In *Colorado Gunsmoke* every effort has been made to sort out the historical facts of these events from the editorial exuberance of the reporters. Where resources contradict each other, footnotes are used to point out the differences. For most stories, the author double-checked the newspapers written at the time as well as various manuscripts. The references listed at the end of each story reflect all source material.

The Virginia Dale stage station, established by Jack Slade in 1862, is still standing and is one of the oldest structures in northern Colorado. The building is located a short distance north of U.S. 287 on a dirt road that runs through private property. Local residents maintain the structure. *Kenneth Jessen*

Slade of Virginia Dale

S tealing horses from stagecoach companies was a common crime in the mid-1800s. The loss of horses was a small problem compared to the delay in schedule. Joseph A. Slade was hired by the Overland Stage Company in 1858 to handle one of its divisions and to put an end to the horse stealing. Slade caught and killed some of the horse thieves, and his actions conformed with public sentiment. Nevertheless, Slade's hiring was a decision the stage company would come to regret.

The legend of Jack Slade claims he carried a Navy percussion revolver and was an excellent marksman. Stories vary greatly as to how many men Joseph "Jack" Slade killed, but Mark Twain placed the figure at twenty-six when he met Slade at Julesburg, Colorado. It is said that one time Slade was approached by a man he did not like, and he remarked to some of his companions who were standing by at the time, "Gentlemen, it is a good twenty-yard shot—I'll clip the third button on his coat!" He did, and the bystanders all admired it, and they attended the man's funeral.

Another time Slade was said to have asked for some brandy from a barkeeper he did not especially care for. The man reached under the counter, but Jack Slade smiled and told him, "None of that! Pass out the high-priced article." The barkeeper had to turn his back to get the better grade of brandy from the shelf behind the bar. When he looked around, he was staring into the muzzle of Slade's pistol. A witness recalled, "And the next instant, he was one of the deadest men that ever lived."

These may be legends or exaggerations of what really happened, but there is one story that has a great deal of credence and that truly sets Jack Slade apart from other men. Jules Beni[1] was the Overland Stage Company's stationmaster at Julesburg, a town named for Beni. Living in the remote northeastern part of Colorado, Beni had very little supervision. Overland coaches

On October 29, 1870, William H. Jackson took this photograph of the Virginia Dale stage station. The arrival of the railroad put the Overland Stage Company out of business between Laramie and Denver around the time this photograph was taken. The actual station is in the background with the livery stable in the foreground. *Colorado Historical Society*

carrying large shipments were being singled out to be robbed, and an official of the Overland Stage Company thought the robberies were an inside job. Jules Beni was suspected of being the mastermind behind the operation,[2] and Jack Slade was hired to replace him.

Beni deeply resented being replaced by Slade, and an animosity grew between the two men. Of their many quarrels, the most serious took place in 1858, culminating in Beni firing his pistol at Slade five times, hitting him every time. Beni, who was standing by the door of his cabin, then took a shotgun and fired its load into Slade's body.[3] Slade was carried into the stage station, bleeding from practically every pore in his body, with thirteen assorted lead slugs in him.[4] Everyone who witnessed the surprise attack agreed that Slade's wounds were so serious that he could not survive. Beni was well satisfied that he had slain his rival and said to the other men, "When he is dead, you can put him in one of these dry-goods boxes and bury him."

Slade overheard Beni's directions and raised himself up from the bunk. He gave the following oath: "I shall live long enough to wear one of your ears on my watch-guard. You needn't trouble yourself about my burial." Beni's response was not recorded.

The Overland coach arrived at this time, carrying the road's superintendent. He found Slade writhing in agony and, upon hearing the story of what had happened, had a scaffold erected immediately. Beni was drawn up by the neck three times by others more than eager to participate. Eventually, Beni's face was ashen from lack of blood. On letting him down for the last time, the superintendent extracted Beni's promise to leave the area permanently.

Slade hung on to life for several weeks and miraculously regained some of his strength. After spending some time in St. Louis for further treatment, he returned to work as the stationmaster of the Julesburg division, but he still carried eight of Beni's slugs inside his body. As the attack had been unprovoked, Slade was advised by his friends to kill Jules Beni at the next opportunity. Warnings were issued to that effect all along the Overland Stage system. However, Slade elected not to hunt down Beni but to let nature take its course.

Although there isn't a known photograph of Joseph A. "Jack" Slade, this likeness has been used over the years to represent him. *Colorado Historical Society*

Jules Beni went about buying and selling cattle in other parts of Colorado. Soon after Slade returned to work, Beni returned to the Julesburg area to recover some of his cattle. He boasted, however, that he was really after Slade to finish him off once and for all. This threat was circulated through the area. Beni even exhibited the pistol with which he proposed to do the job.

At Pacific Springs, on the west end of his division, Slade first heard of Jules Beni's threats and of his return to the area. As Slade traveled toward Julesburg, he was warned all along the route. Slade talked to the military officers at Fort Laramie (north of the present town of Laramie) and decided to follow their advice: the officers told Slade to seek out Beni and to kill him immediately; there would be no peace along the division as long as Jules Beni lived.

At a stage station twelve miles from Fort Laramie, Slade was told that Beni had just passed through the night before. Beni had repeated his threats and had again exhibited his pistol. He planned to wait somewhere along the Overland Stage route to ambush Slade.

Jack Slade acted quickly by sending four of his men ahead to capture and disarm Beni. Slade followed in a coach. As the coach approached the next station at Chansau's ranch, Slade was in the driver's seat. Two of his men came riding toward him at a full gallop. He was informed that Beni was being held at the next station. As the stagecoach pulled up to the station where Beni was being held, Slade jumped down from the box and walked over to several of his men standing in the doorway of the stage station. Slade checked his pistol to see that it was loaded and said, "I want this."

Slade came out of the station and walked over to the corral in the rear where Jules Beni was tied to a post. As soon as Slade saw his enemy, he fired his pistol, trying to put a ball between Beni's eyes. His aim was a little low and the ball struck Beni in the cheek. Beni fell backward and acted as though he had been fatally wounded.

Slade immediately recognized the ruse and told Beni so. He also told Beni that he planned to kill him but would give him the chance to make out a will if he wanted to do so.

Beni said he would like to make out a will, and a passenger on the coach volunteered to draw it up for him. Notes were taken, and a will was drafted in the stage station. The completed

Stagecoaches for the Overland Stage Company looked much like this one photographed in 1867 at Kimball's Station, Utah. These coaches were typically drawn by a six-horse team. *Colorado Historical Society*

will was taken back out to Beni to read and approve. He accepted it, and the man who wrote it returned to the stage station to get a pen and ink. A shot rang out, and by the time the man returned, Jules Beni was slumped in his ropes, dead.[5]

Jack Slade surrendered himself at Fort Laramie. Military authority was the only law in the area. The officers were familiar with his case and, possibly because they had advised Slade to kill Beni, discharged him. The stage company, after its own investigation, signified its judgment on Slade's action by continuing to employ him.

After the stage route was changed from its original course (across Wyoming to Julesburg) to a route south along the Front Range in northern Colorado, Jack Slade was transferred to a newly created division. The place selected for the stage station was in a beautiful valley surrounded by low, forested hills and punctuated with interesting rock formations. The station was established by Slade in June 1862, and he named the location Virginia Dale after his dear wife. Although Jack Slade was as hard a man as the frontier ever produced, he loved his wife dearly. She was a strong, loyal woman, and she stood by her husband through thick and thin.

At Virginia Dale, Slade was recognized as one of the most efficient agents on the entire line. He never failed to get the U.S. mail through on time. Stage robbers and road agents feared him.[6]

Nevertheless, Jack Slade had been in charge of the division and the station for only a little over a year when he was discharged by the Overland Stage Company. The problem was his conduct during his drinking bouts. Under the influence of liquor, he was a terror to his associates.

An early settler in the nearby Big Thompson Valley, Frank Bartholf, told of his first encounter with Slade:

> I received my introduction to Slade over on the Little Thompson at the stage station in the fall of 1862. Slade was coming down over the line from his station at Virginia Dale, and at LaPorte he got drunk. Between LaPorte and Big Thompson station he began firing down through the top of the coach and the four passengers inside rolled out on the prairie. Slade drove into the Big Thompson station at Mariana's[7] on the dead run, and going inside, ordered the agent, a man named Boutwell, to make him a cocktail. A loaded shotgun stood in the corner. Slade picked it up

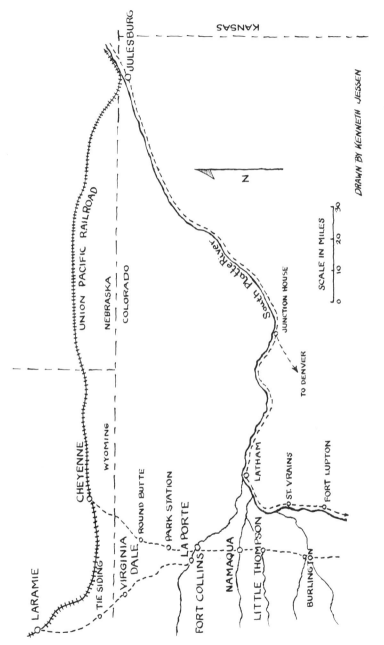

SOME STAGE STOPS AND ROADS IN NORTHERN COLORADO DURING THE 1860's

DRAWN BY KENNETH JESSEN

and cocking both barrels covered Boutwell with it and ordered the drink mixed in a certain manner. Hardly able to hold anything, his hand shook, so Boutwell did as directed. When he had completed the mixture, Slade ordered him to come from behind the counter and place the glass on the muzzle end of the gun, which he did, the two barrels of the gun staring him in the face all the way.

Bartholf then told how Slade drank the concoction and climbed back into the driver's seat. He ran the horses so hard over to the Little Thompson station that one of the animals lay down from exhaustion. Bartholf continued his narrative:

I was keeping the station for my brother-in-law, who had gone up into the hills to bring down his wife. As the stage drove up I went out to unhitch the horses. The driver made some insulting remark to me and I answered him pretty short. Biff! Something struck me across the right eye. I turned quickly and looked straight into the muzzles of two revolvers. I had never seen Slade before, but I realized it once we were introduced. After I went into the stable he walked over to where a couple of young fellows were camped and threatened to steal one of their horses and did kill their dog that was quietly lying under the wagon. Then he kicked their coffee pot over, put out the fire and went off. All this time the two fellows with their guns in hand stood and watched him. He had terrorized them and they dared not lift a finger. Slade afterwards wrote me a letter of apology, saying he thought I was the agent and that he did not allow any of his agents to 'sass him.'

This same year, Slade had quite a bit of trouble with his drivers. The type of individual attracted to the job tended to be wild and reckless. Some drivers also got drunk at every opportunity. One drunken driver had a runaway that resulted in a damaged coach and injured passengers. Slade suspected his driver had purchased his liquor in a store in LaPorte that happened to be owned by one of the stageline's agents. He sent word to the agent not to sell liquor to any of his drivers. The agent replied by saying he would sell to whomever he pleased. This was not the type of reply Jack Slade took lightly. Two nights later when the stage pulled up to the LaPorte station, Slade and three of his men walked into the store and began shooting bottles on the shelves. They caught the agent and tied him up. Next, they opened the faucets on barrels of liquor and molasses. They mixed in flour, and, with the door open, they took turns running in from the street and sliding across the floor. When Slade and his men got tired of this, Slade walked over to the agent and said, "Now, when I tell you not to sell liquor to my men, I mean it."

Another incident involving Jack Slade took place at Mariano Medina's store and saloon at Namaqua on the Big Thompson River near present-day Loveland. One day, when Mariano's fourteen-year-old son Antonio was alone and tending his father's store, in walked Jack Slade. In one of his drunken, wild moods, Slade became abusive. Antonio grabbed his father's Hawken rifle. He aimed it right at Slade and might have pulled the trigger on the cocked weapon if his mother had not knocked the gun up toward the ceiling.

And so, with Slade's reputation as a killer and his intolerable behavior when drunk, the Overland decided to dismiss him. He had outlived his usefulness and was now giving the company a bad name. Robert J. Spotswood was selected to replace Slade as superintendent of the division.

As told so well by Spotswood, "When I received the appointment as superintendent of the division to succeed Slade, my friends in Denver bade me good-bye almost tearfully. It was predicted that I would never return to Denver alive. 'Slade will kill you rather than yield his post,' I was told, but I answered that the killing would have to take place as there was nothing for me to do but go ahead and obey the company's orders."

Spotswood traveled the one hundred miles northwest of Denver to beautiful Virginia Dale, remembering it was named by Jack Slade for his wife. He told Slade why he had come, half anticipating a wild outbreak of emotion. Instead, in an unexpected demonstration of rational behavior, Slade bowed to the will of the company, and he and his wife made Spotswood comfortable. Slade accounted for all of the company's property and turned the station over in good shape. He took with him his horses and mules. He told Spotswood he would go to Virginia City, Montana, and establish himself as a freighter.

After arriving in Virginia City and setting up his business, Jack Slade encountered Nathaniel Pitt Langford in April 1864. At the time, Langford was operating a lumber yard. Slade came in with a team and selected some long boards. He directed the teamster to put the lumber on the bed of the wagon. He then turned and asked Langford, "How long credit will you give me on the purchase?"

Langford answered, "About as long as it will take to weigh the dust."

Slade replied, "That's played out."

Langford explained that he himself could only buy for cash and therefore had to require that his sales be on a cash basis. Slade reacted by calling for the teamster to return the load. As soon as it was replaced, Slade, having thought the situation over, remarked, "Well, I can't get along without the boards anyhow." He then asked that the boards be loaded back onto the wagon.

The verbal battle between Slade and Langford continued as the latter insisted on doing only a cash and carry business. The lumber was unloaded, then reloaded, a third time.

Slade finally said, "Oh well, I guess you'll let me have it."

The reply was immediate and predictable, "Certainly not," said Langford. "Why should I let you have it sooner than another?"

Slade's reply was, "Then I guess you don't know who I am." Langford said that it didn't matter. "Well," in an authoritative tone, "my name is Slade." Langford still didn't recognize who he was dealing with. Jack Slade pressed the issue, "You must have heard of Slade of Virginia Dale?"

"Never before," was Langford's reply.

This answer seemed to insult the man. He rounded up some of his friends who were in a local saloon, then directed them to load up the lumber. To prevent Langford from being killed in what was rapidly becoming a tense situation, a friend of Langford's said he would see that the lumber was paid for the following day.

Slade's acts of violence continued. One of his customs when intoxicated was to mount his horse and ride through Virginia City, stopping at each saloon. He would direct his horse into the saloon and shoot out the lamps and break glasses. He would also toss the gold scales out into the street. The people of Virginia City soon grew tired of this behavior.

There was no official law in the town, only a People's Court composed of the town's responsible citizens. A man with good character served as the judge. Slade stepped over the boundary of human tolerance after an especially violent drunken foray on

After leaving Virginia Dale in Colorado, Joseph A. "Jack" Slade moved to Montana where he constructed this cabin on a ranch near Virginia City. The people in the photograph are not identified. *Western History Department, Denver Public Library*

every saloon in town. He defied the orders of the People's Court to restrain himself in the future and threatened the judge with his derringer.

The local vigilante committee then voted to exterminate Slade. The committee arrested him, and one of its members announced simply, "The Committee has decided upon your execution."

"My execution! My death! My God! Gentlemen, you will not proceed to such extremities," Slade replied. The sentence was repeated, and Slade fell to his knees. He was fully aware of the effect his drunken lawlessness had on the town. He implored the committee to show mercy, saying, "My God! My God! Must I die? Oh, my dear wife. Why can she not be sent for?"

When Slade realized how hopeless the situation was, he sent a messenger to get his wife, who was at their cabin. He also asked that the committee postpone his execution until she arrived. The committee, however, wanted to play it safe, since Virginia Slade had a reputation of her own. It was feared that she might try to free her husband.

The scaffold was nothing more than the gateway to a corral. Jack Slade was placed on a drygoods box, and the noose was tied around his neck. One of Slade's friends threw down his coat and doubled his fists. He said that Jack Slade would be hung over his dead body. The muzzles of many guns changed his mind. Slade was pushed from the box and died.

His body was taken to a hotel and laid out. His wife, mounted on a fast horse, galloped madly into town shortly after the execution. She jumped from the horse and ran to her husband's side. Her cries were mixed with curses directed at those who had ended her husband's life.

Notes

1. Jules Beni's name is also spelled "Reni" by some historians. See Ansel Watrous's *History of Larimer County*, p. 73 or Bill O'Neal's *Encyclopedia of Western Gunfighters*, p. 286.

2. Other historians, including Mark Twain in *Roughing It*, p. 105, added horse theft to Beni's list of crimes.

3. Other accounts place this event at a store and only after Beni and Slade had been hunting each other in Julesburg. Also, it was said Beni was shot during the encounter. See *Roughing It,* p. 105.

4. In the *Encyclopedia of Western Gunfighters* by Bill O'Neal, it is related that Slade got to his feet after the shooting. All historians agree he was hit multiple times by Beni.

5. This account, given in Nathaniel Langford's *Vigilante Days and Ways,* differs materially from other accounts, such as the one given by Mark Twain. Twain wrote that Slade examined Jules Reni to see if he was securely tied, then went to bed. In the morning, Slade used his gun to nip flesh here and there, "occasionally clipping off a finger, while Jules begged him to kill him outright. . . ." According to Twain, Slade killed Reni, then cut off the dead man's ears and placed them in his vest pocket. Slade was said to have carried the ears for some time with great satisfaction. Langford claims this story is false.

6. Slade was said to have been the head of a gang of stage robbers centered near Virginia Dale. It is also said Slade hid the plunder in a rugged mountain called Robbers Roost northeast of the stage station (see Watrous, *History of Larimer County,* p. 190). It would not be logical for Slade to have engaged in such activity, since he had fought hard to eliminate the criminal element along the route of the Overland.

7. Bartholf misspelled the name. It was actually Mariano Medina.

References

Annals of Wyoming 7, no. 2 (October 1930): 306, 375.

Breihan, Carl W. "Captain Joe Slade, the Big Wolf." *Real West* (Fall 1974): 45–49, 80.

Collins, Dabney Otis. *The Hanging of Bad Jack Slade.* Denver: Golden Bell Press, 1963.

Darwin, Wayne. "Who Really Condemned Slade to Hang?" *Western Frontier* (May 1985): 38–43, 58.

Dunning, Harold Marion. *Over Hill and Dale.* Boulder: Johnson Publishing Co., 1956, pp. 576–580.

Gates, Zethyl. *Mariano Medina.* Boulder: Johnson Publishing Co., 1981, pp. 67–68.

Langford, Nathaniel Pitt. *Vigilante Days and Ways.* Bozeman: Montana State University, 1957, pp. 360–376.

Lee, Wayne C. "Julesburg, the Wandering Town." *True West* (March 1983).

Long, James A. "Strange Truth about Jack Slade." *Golden West* (October 1974): 8-10, 45.

O'Dell, Roy P. "Did 'Jack' Slade Really Have Four Ears?" *Quarterly of the National Association and Center for Outlaw and Lawman History* 9, no. 4 (Spring 1985): 16-17.

Patterson, Richard. "Was 'Jack' Slade an Outlaw?" *Quarterly of the National Association and Center for Outlaw and Lawman History* 9, no. 4 (Spring 1985): 14-15.

Shackleford, William Yancy. *Gun-Fighters of the Old West.* Girard, Kansas: Haldeman-Julius Publications, 1943, pp. 11-12.

Twain, Mark. *Roughing It.* Hartford, Conn.: American Publishing Company, 1872, pp. 104-119.

Watrous, Ansel. *History of Larimer County.* Fort Collins: Courier Printing & Publishing Co., 1911, pp. 73-76, 105-106, 189, 191.

The Elephant Corral was one of James Gordon's hangouts. This view looking down Blake Street was taken around 1864 or 1865, just a few years after Gordon shot Jacob Gantz to death on the street. *Colorado Historical Society*

James Gordon Brought to Justice

J ames A. Gordon was a pleasant, likable young man when sober but a murderous ruffian when drunk. Gordon became a landmark in the history of Denver. When he was alive, he was nothing more than a drop in an ocean of disorder sweeping into the Rockies. But hanging from a scaffold on the bank of Cherry Creek, he became a grim signpost to serve notice that law and order was coming to the American West.

The stampede to the Rocky Mountains in 1859 was precipitated by gold. News of the discovery of gold swept across the country and drew countless adventurers. Thousands of gold seekers risked death to travel across the Great American Desert. They came to Denver in wagons, carts, and broughams; on horseback; and on foot. One man even arrived pushing a wheelbarrow.

The trail from the Missouri River was marked by broken wagons and the bleached skeletons of horses and oxen. Mixed in were the lonely graves of emigrants. Goods, such as plows, picks, cookstoves, beds, and pots and pans, littered the dusty trails. These were the items dropped by weary pioneers to lighten their loads.

When young Jim Gordon and his father reached Cherry Creek, all they saw was a village of shacks and tents. Not a single glass window could be found in Denver or its neighbor, Auraria. The cabins all had dirt floors and sod roofs. The streets were deep in dust, pulverized by the weight of wagons, oxen, and horses. A stranger might ask an "old timer" (who had arrived the week before) if the wind blew that way all the time. He might get a dry reply, something like, "No, sometimes it blows the other way."

Denver and Auraria were part of Kansas Territory, and the nearest official law was five hundred blistering miles east across the prairie. There were no sheriffs, judges, or courts appointed by the territory to impede human nature or quick justice.

Jim Gordon was twenty-three years old when his father settled on a ranch a few miles north of Denver in 1860. The younger Gordon had been educated as an engineer. He had wavy blond hair and stood six feet tall. His charming smile was enhanced by an honest look in his blue eyes. His good looks were combined with a winning personality, but only when sober. Young Gordon had no desire for the dull life his father led as a rancher, but chose the turbulent, hurly-burly environment of Denver. He soon fell in with Denver's rougher element.

On Wednesday evening, July 18, 1860, Gordon drank hard and long until he was quite mean. Several times he waved his pistol. In an Arapahoe Street saloon, he wantonly shot down bartender Frank O'Neill. The only offense committed by the bartender was to protest Gordon's wild actions.

The day after the shooting, Gordon's conscience got the best of him. He visited O'Neill and apologized for his actions. Gordon offered to pay all of O'Neill's expenses. The bartender eventually got well.

Gordon's regret was short-lived, however, and he went on another wild, drunken binge two days after the first shooting incident. With two companions, Jim Gordon wandered from one saloon to another, becoming progressively more intoxicated. At a place called the Elephant Corral, Gordon started an argument with Big Phil. The mountain man shrugged off Gordon and his friends, then strolled away. Angered at Big Phil for walking off, Gordon whipped out his revolver and began firing. Some anonymous observer later mentioned that Big Phil went out the back door so fast he passed several bullets!

With gun in hand, Gordon left the Elephant Corral for the Louisiana Saloon on Blake Street. For amusement, he fired twice at a dog but missed. At the Louisiana, Gordon became peeved when the bartender did not put water out with the whiskey. In a drunken frenzy, he flung a bottle at the line of bottles behind the counter, smashing half a dozen or so. The patrons ran for the door. Gordon blocked the way of one man and knocked him to the floor. The man was an elderly German emigrant from Leavenworth, Kansas, named Jacob Gantz. Gordon offered the terrified Gantz a drink, but his offer was politely refused. Gantz got to his feet and ran quickly out the door of the saloon into the street. The drunken Gordon managed to outrun the old man and once more flung him down. He kneeled on the German's chest and held him by the hair. Gordon pointed his pistol at Gantz's head.

The old man pleaded for his life, saying, "For God's sake, don't kill me." Gordon cocked his weapon and pulled the trigger. The only sound was the hammer striking an empty chamber. Gordon again cocked his revolver and pulled the trigger. The hammer clicked harmlessly. Twice more the helpless victim was subjected to this torture. On the fifth try, the gun discharged. The bullet crashed into the German's brain, and he died almost instantly. Gordon got to his feet and rejoiced, "I've killed a damned Dutchman and don't care, but would like to kill more."

Well-known Denver gambler Charley Harrison learned of Gordon's binge. Harrison immediately rode out to the Gordon ranch and informed the boy's parents of the shooting. He learned that Jim hadn't been home for over a week. Harrison promised to do all he could for their son, then headed back to town. The gambler quickly learned that an enraged mob was looking for Gordon as their "honored" guest at a hanging. In the meantime, Harrison found Gordon fast asleep under some bushes near the Cibola Hall. The gambler got one of his horses and helped Gordon to escape.[1]

The young murderer was sighted galloping toward Fort Lupton. Word of Gordon's location reached Denver, and a man named Babcock gathered a half dozen men and rode in pursuit. Gordon took refuge at the Blake and Williams ranch at Fort Lupton. Babcock and his men learned where Gordon was hiding and surrounded the house, but Gordon managed to dash for freedom. One of the members of the posse, however, got near enough to wound Gordon's mount. Dusk came, and Gordon was able to elude them by hiding in the brush along the banks of the South Platte River. The posse was forced to return to Denver empty handed.

Gordon made it to Box Elder station where he purchased a mule. He crossed eastern Colorado by riding south, avoiding well-traveled roads.

With James Gordon was still at large, a highly agitated public meeting was held in Denver, and a large sum of money was raised as a bounty for capturing Gordon. W. H. Middaugh agreed to track down the killer. For ten days he hunted Gordon along the South Platte River. Clues led Middaugh to Leavenworth, Kansas, where he was appointed a deputy U.S. marshal. Along with another deputy, he set out to find his man.

James Gordon made the error of writing to a friend in Denver. The man who promised to deliver the letter accidentally met Middaugh. It was this type of lead that Middaugh so desperately needed, and it was in this way he learned his man was hiding at Bent's Fort.

Before Middaugh could reach the fort, however, Gordon joined a forty-team wagon convoy and headed south for Texas. At the fort, Middaugh learned of Gordon's destination, and he and the other deputy took off after the convoy. The two law officers caught up with the wagon train and learned a man meeting Gordon's description had ridden off on his own for Fort Gibson. Subsequently, Gordon had joined four other men to travel safely through the Cherokee country of Oklahoma.

The two deputies purchased a fresh team for their light wagon. They traced Gordon to a small town where they found that they were only a day behind him. By asking everyone they met about him, they learned from a farmer that Gordon was now only a half hour ahead of them.

While riding down a wagon road, the deputies came upon a man grazing his mule in a small meadow beside the trail. The man was Gordon. Middaugh disarmed Gordon and recovered a Colt .44-caliber revolver as well as a derringer. Jim Gordon, having thought he had made a clean getaway, was visibly shaken at having been captured.

At the nearest blacksmith shop, Gordon was fitted with irons. Instead of heading diagonally back across Colorado to Denver, Middaugh took his prisoner to Leavenworth. What the newly appointed deputy marshal could not have foreseen was that Kansas authorities would raise legal technicalities over returning the fugitive to Denver. Middaugh also could not have known he would have to save Gordon from a lynch mob.

There were many German settlers in Leavenworth, and some had known Jacob Gantz. His reputation as a quiet, hardworking man who was brutally murdered by James Gordon had caused a lot of excitement in Leavenworth. When Gordon was brought into town, it didn't take long before hundreds of men gathered in the streets, and talk began about lynching

Middaugh's prisoner. The mob surrounded the courthouse in which legal points as to who had jurisdiction over the Gordon case were being argued. The presiding judge decided in favor of simply letting Gordon go free.

The fury of the mob outside grew in intensity, and a chorus of "Hang him! Hang him!" echoed through the streets. Mayor McDowell tried to calm the crowd from the balcony of the courthouse and argued in favor of law and order. His words were to no avail, and it was decided that Gordon should be locked in jail for his own safety. McDowell was a courageous man and, in the face of insurmountable odds, organized an impromptu posse. Middaugh was one of its members. With Gordon in the center, the posse fought its way down the street to the jail.

As night came, the crowd grew larger and more unruly. Bonfires were lit as peddlers hawked food. The streets of Leavenworth were alive with yelling men demanding the hanging of James Gordon. An attack on the jail seemed imminent, and McDowell again tried to appeal to the mob.

It was finally agreed that Gordon would be turned over to Middaugh and taken to the Planter's House, a hotel in town, pending an adjustment of the earlier ruling to set the prisoner free. The jailer was anxious to get Gordon out of the building.

Middaugh, the deputy, and a few other posse members began to move the murderer to the hotel. The howling mob soon closed in on the men, and twice a rope noose was thrown over Gordon's neck. Middaugh flung the rope off the first time, and the deputy sawed the rope with a knife the second time, while Gordon was on his knees. The group struggled against the mob as they slowly made their way to the Planter's House. Every stitch of clothing was torn from the prisoner.[2] Gordon was so battered, bruised, and terrified that he begged again and again to be shot on the spot. Fortunately, a group of soldiers came to rescue the posse and their prisoner.

A second hearing took place. Much to Middaugh's utter amazement, local authorities refused to relinquish Gordon for the trip back to Denver, but still held the murderer in jail. This forced Middaugh to return empty handed. In Denver, the weary marshal was welcomed as a hero for his persistence in trying to extradite Gordon. More money was raised, and three witnesses to the Gantz murder, along with affidavits detailing every aspect of the case, were turned over to Middaugh. With the witnesses, Middaugh boarded the stagecoach for the hot, dusty trip back to Leavenworth.

This time the evidence was great enough for Leavenworth officials to conclude that Gordon should stand trial in Denver. Middaugh, Gordon, and three guards boarded a Denver-bound stage, but before they had traveled a hundred miles, they were recalled to Leavenworth and Gordon was charged by a Leavenworth judge with stealing his mule. Once this problem was settled, Gordon was again released to the custody of Marshal Middaugh, but now there were only two seats left on the stage to Denver. This forced Middaugh to chain himself to his prisoner. During the long trip neither man got much sleep.

At two o'clock in the morning, the stage rolled into Denver, and Middaugh was finally able to deliver his prisoner. It was September 28, and Middaugh had spent two months tracking down Gordon. In the process, he traveled more than 3,000 miles.

Judge A. C. Hunt presided over the trial of James A. Gordon. The court and the prosecution were men of high character but with no legal training or territorial sanction. In a grove of cottonwood trees below Wazee Street, the trial was held before a thousand people. The court did everything to give the accused a fair trial, and the defense was encouraged to put up the strongest possible arguments. The proceedings were not hurried, and the Gordon trial lasted several days, ending on October 2, 1860. The jury of twelve brought in a verdict of murder, and Gordon was sentenced to hang on Saturday, October 6. The verdict was submitted to the crowd for their approval, to which Gordon responded with a bow.

At the appointed time, a buggy carrying the prisoner arrived at the scaffold on the east bank of Cherry Creek. Guards surrounded the gallows to prevent any last-minute rescue. At Gordon's request, Middaugh was placed in charge of the hanging. The prisoner knelt in prayer while several thousand spectators uncovered their heads. Moments later James Gordon was dead.

Notes

1. This story varies. Harrison is not implicated in some versions. For example, in *Denver's Murderers*, p. 21, William Raine says Gordon fled to his father's ranch and obtained a horse.

2. As incredible as it seems, this aspect of Gordon's rescue can be confirmed in more than one source.

References

Casy, Lee, ed. *Denver Murders*. New York: Duell, Sloan, and Pearce, 1946, pp. 13–31.

Smiley, Jerome C. *History of Denver.*. Denver: Old American Publishing Co, 1901, pp. 343–346.

Zamonski, Stanley W. and Teddy Keller. *The '59er's.* 3d ed. Frederick, Colo.: Platte 'N Press Books, 1983, pp. 121–127.

Perkin, Robert L. *The First Hundred Years*. New York: Doubleday & Co., 1959, pp. 178–179.

When this photograph was taken in April 1861, a crowd had gathered at the Criterion Saloon to watch a tightrope walker. At the time, one of the owners was Denver gambler Charley Harrison. During his brief two years in Denver, Harrison shot two men to death. *Colorado Historical Society*

Denver Gambler Charley Harrison

C harley Harrison came to Denver in the summer of 1859, just as the town was getting its start. Harrison was a gambler by trade and had drifted in from Salt Lake City. He rode into town on a stolen pony acquired during his flight from a Mormon posse. He took a room at the Elephant Corral, sold his horse, and used the money for new clothes. He rented a table and was back in business.

Always well groomed and always the gentleman, Harrison typified the cool, calculating gambler of the American West. He dressed in black and his "authority" was carried as a pair of pearl-handled Colts on his hips. Marked cards, loaded dice, fixed roulette wheels, and rigged games were below his dignity. He was a businessman and never drank while working. His nimble fingers and quick moves of the cards were all Harrison needed to separate some greenhorn from his cash.

Harrison's life and times soon became associated with the famous Criterion Hall. This two-story frame building housed Denver's most ornate hotel and dining room. The Criterion also provided dancing and gambling. Windows were etched with delicate floral designs, and the liquor cellar was well stocked. A handsome sign hung over the front of the building, which added an air of luxury to the otherwise primitive settlement along Cherry Creek.

Ed Jump, the proprietor of the Criterion Hall, ran the following ad in the *Rocky Mountain News*:

> Criterion Saloon and Restaurant
> Larimer Street, Denver
> Ed Jump, Proprietor
>
> I constantly keep on hand all kinds of liquors, cigars, etc. You will find nothing but the best in my bar. My dining room is

supplied with all the delicacies of the country. One hundred day boarders can be accommodated.

William Byers, editor of the *Rocky Mountain News*, praised Ed Jump with the following editorial:

> If there are any so credulous as to believe that we have no good living in this country, we advise them to drop in at the Criterion presided over by the prince of landlords, Ed Jump.

The Criterion Hall was irresistible to Charley Harrison, so he purchased part ownership from Ed Jump. To try to improve upon the hall may have seemed like a case of gilding the lily, but after Harrison redecorated the Criterion, it had no equal in the territory. It also had a new proprietor who was frequently in the midst of controversy and violence.

The First Division of the Utah Army, under the command of Colonel Morrison, marched into Denver after being caught in a violent rainstorm. The storm had caused severe flooding in Denver and Auraria. The bleary-eyed, dirty troops slogged through the mud in a listless struggle to reach their stopping point. The Colonel decided to get his troops into a temporary camp on the south side of Cherry Creek. In the process, he had the Larimer Street bridge reinforced for the safety of his men.

Once again, it started to rain, and rain it did for three days. When the water receded, residents once again began removing mud and debris from their homes and businesses.

When the warm July sun finally broke through, the one thought on the minds of the soldiers was to have some fun. It had been a long time since these men had seen the clean inside of a parlor house or felt the companionship of a woman. Denver was a wide-open town filled with many "houses of pleasure." A half-dozen bedraggled soldiers stomped into Ada LaMont's bordello and immediately tried to force themselves on her girls. True, the ladies did earn their living from the amorous advances of men, but not from those who acted in such a brash manner. Screaming, the girls fled into the street.

Alcohol had slowed the soldiers' reflexes, and they made no attempt to follow the fleet-footed girls. Instead, they turned their attention to the rows of liquor behind the bar. The madam pleaded with the men to leave. Just as further destruction to

Ada's place seemed certain, Charley Harrison and three companions entered. In his typically cool manner, he admonished the soldiers by saying, "We don't have any objections to you fellows having a little fun. A drink and a lady's smile once in a while can do a man a whale of a lot of good. But there's no need for you to wreck the place." It was obvious that trouble was brewing. Harrison and his companions were armed and the soldiers weren't. Harrison made a magnanimous offer. He suggested that each soldier take what liquor he could carry and leave. Harrison said he would cover the cost. Of the six, five grabbed a couple of bottles, and the last man departed with an extra pair tucked under his arms.

On that day, Charley was worn out from protecting the Criterion from flood damage, and his nerves may have been frayed from the encounter with the soldiers. He went to the Cibola Hall for a drink and some friendly conversation. He began to talk with friends who were playing poker.

One of the players was a Negro named "Professor" Charles Stark. He seldom carried a gun but was an expert with his Bowie knife. He used the knife to do anything from trimming his nails to cutting his food. He was known as "Professor" because of his sharp clothes. He often wore a starched, white shirt and a tailored, black suit. Stark claimed to be Mexican; however, others knew him as a former Missouri slave. He was a gambler and at times worked as a blacksmith. Stark was well liked because of his good nature and fine appearance.

Apparently, the game was not going too well for Stark. He spied Charley Harrison and called to him, "Hey, Charley, you're honest, but these goddamn fellows are swindlers."

Harrison was on edge and a little touchy. He snapped back, "Who are you to address me as 'Charley' and these gentlemen as 'swindlers'?"

Professor Stark may not have meant anything by his remark, but Harrison's reply made his blood boil. He kicked his chair across the room as he got to his feet and yelled at Harrison, "Damn your stinking hide. I'll show you who the hell I am." Stark continued his verbal assault on Harrison as he slowly got closer. Harrison held his ground against the bar. Stark drew his knife, a weapon many said could pin a butterfly's wings back at twenty paces.

"Put down the knife, you fool!" Harrison warned.

William Newton Byers founded the *Rocky Mountain News* and remained its editor for nineteen years. He was not afraid to criticize Denver's lawless element. His life was saved in July 1860 by gambler Charley Harrison. *Colorado Historical Society*

Stark lunged at Harrison again and again with the formidable Bowie knife. Harrison ducked and dodged its razor-sharp edge. Stark pressed for the kill, and Harrison drew his gun and fired. As Stark began to slump to the floor from the first round, Harrison continued to pump lead into the Professor until all six chambers of his Colt were empty.[1]

Everyone in the room either ducked behind the bar or left the building. Stark lay bleeding on the floor. One of the spectators, peeking from behind the bar, noticed that he was still alive. Stark was carried to a small frame building that served as Denver's hospital. He was examined by a doctor who predicted his recovery. Stark had been hit in the right thigh, the shoulder, and the chest. On July 21, 1860, the Professor died. Charley Harrison was not even arrested, possibly because of the growing bitterness over the slave question or the many rough friends he had collected.

On July 25, 1860, editor William Byers let fly at Harrison:

> Prof. Stark, the Mexican Negro, who was shot on the 12th by the gambler, Charley Harrison, died on the night of the 21st from the effect of his wounds. From the facts that have transpired since the shooting, we are led to think that the act was wanton and unprovoked; in short a cold blooded murder—if called by its right name—scarcely less enormous than the several others that have occurred recently.
>
> The man who has shot down an unarmed[2] man, and then repeats his shots, while his victim withers at his feet, until the charges in his pistol are exhausted—even if justified in the first act, is unfit to live in, and an unsafe member of a civilized community.

Byers continued his assault against Denver's rough element. He warned that such acts of violence would no longer be tolerated and that people would take the law into their own hands. Harrison and his cohorts at the Criterion had been called out.

The boys at the Criterion were incensed over this editorial, although Charley Harrison seemed unrattled. He had been denounced by experts before and realized that any attempt at direct action against William Byers would only cause the town to turn against him and his lucrative business. A crowd of his cronies, however, declared that they were not going to just

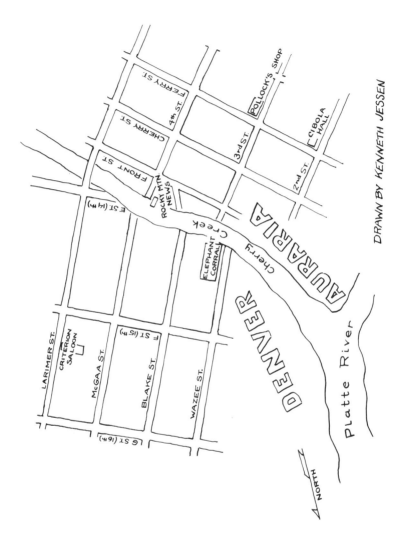

DRAWN BY KENNETH JESSEN

sit by and let the *Rocky Mountain News* print whatever it wanted.

Led by Carroll Wood and George Steele on July 31, 1860, a number of men from the Criterion moved to carry out their threats and to put an end to the "nosy" editor. The delegation burst into the newspaper office. Wood, with a pistol in his hand, uttered a series of what were recorded as "vile oaths." He then grabbed Byers by the collar and thrust his pistol into the editor's face. He demanded that Byers follow him back to the Criterion. During the commotion, some of the printers ran upstairs into the attic.[3]

Byers backed around his office slowly until the Criterion gang was below the trapdoor to the attic. He continued talking, trying to cool the men's tempers, and agreed to go see Charley Harrison. Wood aimed his gun at Byers's head, then lowered it, only to raise the weapon again. Wood was clearly undecided. After a moment of silence, the click-click of cocking guns distracted Wood and his men. They looked up to see several guns pointing down at them.

Nevertheless, William Byers followed Wood and his friends peacefully back to the Criterion. Harrison was behind the bar and was angered at what his troops had done. He grabbed Wood by the arm and demanded, "What in hell do you mean by this?"

The baffled Wood replied, "We brought Byers here for you to settle with. He called you a murderer."

Harrison then led Byers through the gambling hall into a back room, leaving Wood and the rest of the gang behind. He handed the editor a pistol and showed him to the rear door. He told Byers to return to this office and "be ready for the sons of a bitches."

Following Harrison's advice, Byers returned to the *Rocky Mountain News* office[4] and barricaded the windows and doors. With Byers were several other men, including Jack Merrick. They didn't have to wait long before George Steele rode toward the building on horseback. As he passed at a full gallop, he fired through the window. Steele made what were termed "indecent gestures" at the occupants, then fired again. Merrick replied with a shotgun and hit Steele in the back and the hip. The wounded man slumped in his saddle but managed to get out of range. Merrick also exchanged shots with Wood, but neither man was hit.

This is how the *Rocky Mountain News* building looked in 1864 just prior to the Cherry Creek flood. The structure was built in 1860. *Colorado Historical Society*

On Ferry Street, at the home of his mistress, Steele pulled up and dismounted. He told the woman what had happened. She tended to his wounds, which were minor. Steele mounted his horse with a shotgun in hand. He headed out of town to escape capture but had a change of mind. Wheeling his horse about, he recrossed the Platte River bridge, heading toward the Criterion.

Marshal Tom Pollock heard the shots and ran out of his blacksmith shop on Third Street. Heavily bearded, with long red hair, he worked variously as a blacksmith, a cabinet maker, a realtor, a horse trader, and an undertaker. Pollock mounted his horse, shotgun in hand, and saw Steele riding toward him. The horses continued to pound toward each other. When the two men were well within range of each other, they fired almost at the same time.

Pollock unloaded with both barrels into Steele, while the buckshot from the latter's gun completely missed the marshal. One of the blasts hit Steele in the head. He fell from his horse, struggled to get to his feet, then crumpled into the dusty street. He died later that day.

A few months later, in late 1860, Denver became a tinderbox over the slavery issue brewing in the South. Most of the fights between pro-North and pro-South factions were harmless, but several resulted in death. Outside of the Elephant Corral, a brawl between Andy Goff and James Cockron resulted in Cockron beating Goff with his revolver. Goff was soon unconscious, and it was clear that Cockron was about to kill his adversary.

Sheriff Ned Wynkoop and Charley Harrison were inside the Elephant Corral when the disturbance broke out. The two men moved quickly to break up the one-sided battle and to prevent yet another death on Denver's streets. It took Charley's own six-shooter to bring Cockron under control.

"Drop that gun and clear out of here or I'll lock you up," threatened Wynkoop. Cockron and his friends went down the street, while Harrison got a doctor to tend to the badly beaten Andy Goff. Harrison even paid the medical bill.

But Harrison was not done with Cockron's friends. One of them, James Hill, was an imposing figure at six-foot-two. He looked wild, had shaggy hair, and wore heavy, black whiskers. A typical frontiersman, he was fearless. He had shown his bravery against horse thieves just a few months earlier.

This drawing of Charley Harrison was done by H. Ray Baker for *Rocky Mountain Life* in 1948. It is based on written descriptions of Harrison combined with Mr. Baker's own imagination. *Western History Department, Denver Public Library*

Making the rounds of Denver's watering holes, Hill arrived at the Criterion. Charley Harrison was returning to the bar to join newspaperman Cyrus McLaughlin and a few other friends.

A commotion erupted as Hill shouted to the bartender, "You son of a bitch! Who the hell do you think you are tellin' me when I've had enough?"

Harrison, upon hearing this, moved in quickly, but Sheriff Wynkoop got to Hill first. Wynkoop tried to calm Hill down by saying, "Easy does it, Jim. No need of stormin' up the place. There's women present and . . ."

Hill grabbed the sheriff and yelled, "Who's askin' you for advice?" This was followed by a few choice obscenities.

The sheriff shook free and warned Hill about his foul mouth. Hill pulled out his gun, but so did Wynkoop. The two men were sparring verbally when a friend of Hill's approached and asked Hill if he would have a drink with him. Hill eased his gun down, and Harrison guided Hill back to the bar, offering to buy drinks for the men.

The bartender suggested to Hill that he go outside for a little fresh air, a suggestion to which Harrison readily agreed. At that, Hill responded in anger to the bartender, "I won't go anywhere with you or any other son of a bitch."

Harrison warned Hill that he wouldn't put up with having one of his employees called such a name. To that Hill replied, "I'll call him as I damn well please and you ain't any better, you dirty bastard." Hill reached for his gun, and as he did, Harrison seized his gun hand. Simultaneously, Harrison drew his Colt with his free hand and fired at point blank range into Hill's midsection. Harrison's gun spoke again and again until Hill had received four slugs, and he fell to the floor.

Harrison slowly let his weapon fall to the floor beside Hill's body, and as he did, he remarked, "No man is going to call any of my employees a son of a bitch." In a reflective mood, he continued, "Just my damn luck to have this happen in my house."

At three o'clock the next morning, Monday, November 26, Hill died from the multiple gunshot wounds inflicted by Charley Harrison. Harrison regretted his actions, but held fast that he would do it again under the same circumstances.

A warrant was made out for Harrison's arrest, but he refused to surrender. The only law in Denver was the People's Court, and Harrison feared it would end up as a lynching. He got some of his men together and barricaded himself in the Criterion. Hill had had a number of friends, and soon a mob grew under the leadership of Joseph Wolf. Wolf served on the staff of the *Rocky Mountain News* and was a man of some influence. Using a wagon as a platform, he worked the mob into a frenzy. He demanded that Harrison be hung.

Young Asa Middaugh had listened to this and realized how dangerous the situation was. As the crowd moved out, he mounted his horse and galloped across the Cherry Creek bridge. He met his father, the town marshal, and the two rode as hard as they could for Larimer Street.

As they arrived at the Criterion, the mob was coming down the street. The marshal used his wagon to block the way. He shouted at the crowd that he would see that law and order would be preserved. He realized he was not succeeding, but he continued to talk, telling the crowd that Harrison was most likely well armed and that many people would die if they tried to storm the Criterion. The marshal said, "Violence isn't going to get you anywhere. Give me a few minutes, and I'll have Harrison under arrest."

The mob finally began to yield to the marshal's request. Some demanded that they be allowed to go into the Criterion with him. He pointed to his twenty-year-old son, Asa, saying that was all the help he needed. Father and son went to the door of the Criterion and knocked. After a minute or so, Harrison answered and asked them to enter. As he walked in, Marshal Middaugh counted around seventy-five heavily armed men.

Harrison broke the silence between himself and his guests by asking, "Is this a friendly call, Marshal, or is it against the law to open on Sunday?"

The marshal took out an official paper and presented it to Harrison saying, "I have here a warrant for your arrest, Charley, and I'd like you to submit peaceably—to save your skin and others as well."

Harrison's response was predictable: "Self defense, Marshal. He drew first."

"All right, you'll have a chance to prove that in court," continued Middaugh. "I want you to surrender to me." Harrison finally agreed, but only after the marshal vowed to protect him with his own life. Harrison was kept between the marshal and his own son as they got into the wagon. The crowd looked on.

Thanksgiving came and went. On Tuesday, December 4, 1860, the People's Court convened and placed Charley Harrison on trial for the murder of James Hill. Almost all of Denver's businesses were closed for the event. The People's Court consisted of prominent men but lacked any formal authority. Its decisions were directed by common sense rather than legal expertise. Harrison was represented by four prominent men from different occupations.

The proceedings began when Judge William M. Slaughter said, "The People of Denver charge Charles Harrison with the crime of murder, in killing with a pistol, or other deadly weapon, James Hill, at the City of Denver on the twenty-fifth of November, 1860."

A jury was selected, consisting of a civil engineer, a realtor, a businessman, a banker, an actor, and others. A great deal of the testimony during the trial centered around whether or not Hill was armed, and if so, how he used his gun. Many discrepancies came out during the course of the trial, pivoting on whether Hill drew his gun first. What turned the tide in favor of Harrison were accounts from witnesses who attended to Hill's wounds. Apparently Hill admitted drawing first on Harrison. Also, two witnesses heard Hill threaten to kill Harrison even before he entered the Criterion. One account related that Hill said, "I'm going to see this guy Charley Harrison. He's a friend of mine, see? I'm a friend of his. But if he says he's not a friend of mine, then this is." According to the testimony, Hill then put his hand on his pistol.

It was after six in the evening when the jury filed out. After fourteen hours of deliberation, the jury was hung on a vote of ten to two for acquittal. Judge Slaughter dismissed the jury, and the four self-styled defense "attorneys" asked for another trial. The prosecution, on the other hand, preferred not to ask for a new trial, and the case against Charley Harrison was dropped.

Toward the end of the summer of 1861, Harrison was involved in a series of disturbances between his own Criterion gang, which was sympathetic with the South, and soldiers posted in Denver from the Union Army. In a trial that lasted two weeks, Harrison was charged for complicity in a rebellion against the authority of the Union Army. The gambler realized he was all through in Denver. He was found guilty and, on September 17, paid his fine and took the required oath of allegiance to the United States of America. Two days later, he sold his interest in the Criterion and boarded an eastbound stage, never to be seen again in Denver.

Notes

1. The number of bullets fired into Stark's body by Harrison varies in different accounts. Other versions of this story say Stark was hit three times. See *The '59er's*, p. 120 or *The First Hundred Years*, p. 179. The argument between Harrison and Stark had been reported to have been over the issue of Stark's race and the prejudice Harrison had against Negroes.

2. William Byers later retracted the statement that Stark was unarmed and, based on eyewitness accounts, acknowledged that Stark lunged at Harrison two or three times before the latter fired.

3. Other accounts say only one of the employees got into the attic and that a single rifle was inserted through a floor joist. See *The First Hundred Years.*

4. Other accounts say that Harrison escorted Byers back to his office and that Steele shouted, "Damn it to hell! Charley's letting the bastard go!' See *The '59er's*, p. 136.

References

Perkin, Robert L. *The First Hundred Years*. New York: Doubleday & Co. Inc., 1959, pp. 179-181.

Smiley, Jerome, ed. *History of Denver*. Denver: Old American Publishing Co., 1901, pp. 343-349.

Zamonski, Stanley W. and Teddy Keller. *The '59er's*. 3d ed. Frederick, Colo.: Platte 'N Press Books, 1983.

Thomas Tobin, a scout for the U.S. Army, was asked by Colonel Tappan of Fort Garland to bring in the heads of the Espinosas. The Espinosas had been on a killing spree to rid the area of Anglos. Tobin carried out his orders. *Western History Department, Denver Public Library*

He Brought Back Their Heads

D uring the 1860s, the Anglos were the newcomers to the southern part of Colorado and northern New Mexico. Their intrusion was resented by some of the established Mexican families. One family, the Espinosas, took it upon itself to resist the Anglos. The Espinosas claimed that some of their land had been taken by Anglos without compensation. Another story tells that one of their children was killed by Anglos and their sheep run off.

The Espinosas lived in Cucheti, New Mexico, then moved to the San Luis Valley and settled in San Rafael on Conejos Creek. The two Espinosa brothers, José and Vivian, began stealing horses. In the spring of 1863, they stopped a wagon in New Mexico between Santa Fe and Galisteo. The wagon was loaded with goods belonging to a priest stationed in Galisteo who also operated a little store. The Espinosas tied up the teamster and stole goods from the wagon. They then tied the teamster to the wagon tongue and started the team off at a gallop. Fortunately, the priest was out riding and was able to stop the runaway wagon. After the teamster told the priest the details of what had happened, General Carlton in Santa Fe was informed. The robbers were identified as the Espinosa brothers.

General Carlton, in turn, informed Captain Eaton at Fort Garland, and soldiers were sent out to San Rafael to capture the Espinosa brothers. A lieutenant, a deputy U.S. marshal, a sergeant, and fifteen soldiers went to the Espinosa cabin and acted as though they were recruiting for the U.S. Army. When Vivian Espinosa showed no interest in the matter, the lieutenant grabbed him and said he was a prisoner. Espinosa answered, "No, I am not," and jumped into the cabin where he and his brother grabbed their weapons. They killed one soldier, scattered the rest with gunfire, and escaped into the Sangre de Cristo Mountains.

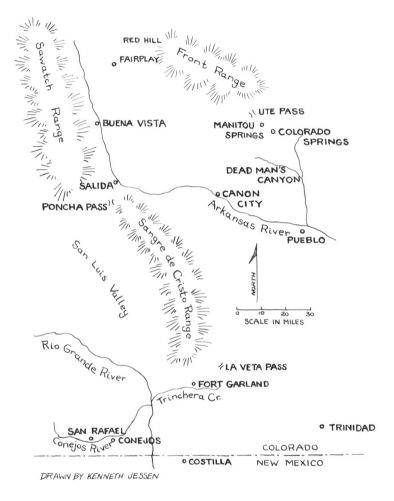

DRAWN BY KENNETH JESSEN

During the following weeks, the Espinosas began a reign of terror unlike any seen in Colorado. The brothers embarked upon a self-styled mission to kill as many Anglos as possible. Their first victim was William Bruce, who lived on Hardscrabble Creek near Canon City. Bruce had been alone at his sawmill and failed to return to his family when expected. A search was made, and Bruce's body was found, shot through the heart.

Henry Harkens was next. He was one of the kindest men in the Fountain Creek area. He was always ready to help anyone in trouble and was known as "Uncle" Harkens. He had moved from Buckskin in 1861 when he was in his mid-fifties. He joined three other men to set up a sawmill in a small canyon called Saw Mill Gulch, about ten miles west of Fountain.

On Wednesday, March 19, 1863, Harkens worked all day on a cabin while his partners worked at the mill a short distance away or on the road leading to the mill. At the end of the day, two of the men returned to the cabin and told Harkens they were going down to see how the road improvements were coming along. Harkens began to cook supper for the men.

The Espinosas were hidden on a small bluff about a quarter of a mile away. When they saw two of the men leave, they rode down to the cabin and shot Harkens in the middle of the forehead. They then took an axe and split his head open from the top of his mouth. Blows to the side of his head left his skull in pieces.

When the other men returned to the cabin for their dinner, they didn't see any light. Instead, they saw Harkens lying on the ground just six feet from the cabin. As the men approached, they saw how brutally he had been murdered. Thinking the killers were still close by, one man drew his revolver and, using the gun barrel, cautiously pushed aside the blanket that served as the cabin's door. Inside, everything had been dumped on the floor, including a sack of flour. A suitcase had been slashed open and its contents scattered about. Due to the nature of the killing, the men believed this to be the work of Indians.

A spot on a little knoll under a sheltering pine tree was selected, and a grave was dug in the rocky soil. Once the hole was complete, small logs were used to line the grave and form a primitive casket. The casket was lined with fragrant boughs, and "Uncle" Harkens was laid to rest. Little poles were placed over the top to form a cover. The soil was replaced, and a small wooden marker was made. It read, "Henry Harkens, Murdered Wednesday Eve., March 19th, 1863." The name of the canyon was subsequently changed to Dead Man's Canyon.

A sheriff and his deputy came by just as the grave was being dug. They had been following the trail of the Espinosas since William Bruce was killed. At the time they were not sure who was committing the murders. From the sawmill they followed the murderers to Colorado City. From there, the trail led to Manitou Springs and over Ute Pass. After finding the body of J. D. Addleman on his ranch in South Park, the lawmen lost the trail and returned home.

A couple of days later, the Espinosas cut down four more men around Red Hill in South Park. One of the men was the brother of Lieutenant George Shoup, a prominent South Park resident. A prospector named Bill Carter fell victim on his claim in South Park. Carter was robbed of his gun, money, and clothing. A couple of California Gulch residents named Lehman and Seyga were killed near Red Hill as they were returning from Denver.

South Park residents didn't know who the killers were, and no one dared to venture out on the roads by day or night. It was thought that Confederate guerrillas had attacked Colorado. No stranger was above suspicion. One poor fellow from California Gulch ran from Red Hill to Fairplay to escape an angry posse. A Methodist minister, "Father" John Dyer, recognized him and was able to save the man by using his own body as a shield from the posse.

A fellow named Baxter was hiding with a family near Fairplay. A posse surrounded the home and demanded Baxter's surrender, thinking he was responsible for the killings. The family refused to release him until several shots were fired, killing a mule. The posse then took Baxter into Fairplay and hung him without a trial. But the murders continued, and it soon became apparent that Baxter hadn't been responsible for them.

For South Park residents, the first clue as to the identity of the murderers came from a man named Metcalf who was shot as he was hauling lumber down the road from Alma to Fairplay. Fortunately, the bullet was stopped by a thick wad of papers he was carrying in his vest pocket. Metcalf saw the two Mexicans as his frightened team took off at a dead run. He informed local authorities in Fairplay, and a posse of seventeen men was organized. Finally, the connection was made between the South Park murders and the Espinosa brothers.

Under the leadership of Captain John McCannon, every part of South Park was searched. By dividing the posse into smaller groups, McCannon was able to pick up the trail of the two murderers. A couple of horses were discovered on the south side of a gulch. McCannon ordered his men to surround the area. After a short time, José Espinosa came out of a willow thicket and began taking the hobble off his horse. One of the posse members fired. The bullet broke the second rib on José's right side. A shotgun also was fired at José but the pellets hit his horse. A third shot was placed between José's eyes. Vivian Espinosa was flushed out but was mistaken for a posse member in the confusion. He escaped and managed to reach San Rafael.

Back at his home, Vivian picked up his twelve-year-old nephew and continued his bloody rampage in Colorado.

At this time, Governor John Evans was traveling in the Conejos area. He had received a threatening letter from the Espinosas saying that the murders were intended as retaliation against the seizure of their family land. They wanted Evans to pay for the land in exchange for stopping the killings.[1] Vivian and his nephew spied Evans's camp but either failed to recognize the governor or left for fear of being detected.

On September 5, 1863, Vivian Espinosa and his nephew attacked a man and a woman from Trinidad. The woman was a Mexican on her way to Costilla to visit relatives. Just as their buggy was entering a canyon near the Sangre de Cristo Mountains, the Espinosas fired on them. One of their two mules was wounded, but the couple drove as fast as they could until the animal died. The Espinosas overtook them, killing the other mule. The man ran up a mountainside with the Espinosas in pursuit while the woman hid herself behind a big rock.

A couple of Mexicans drove up in a wagon, and the terrified woman came out of hiding. She told one of them, Pedro Garcia, what had happened. Garcia told her to get into his wagon and he would protect her. The woman hid in the wagon box. The Espinosas were unable to capture the man they were following and returned to the road. In the distance, they saw the wagon and called, "What people? Answer quick or we will fire on you. We are the Espinosas."

Garcia answered, "Mexicans."

Vivian Espinosa then asked, "Did you meet or see a gringo running down the road?" Garcia answered that he did see a man running down the side of the mountain, and he motioned for Espinosa to go back. Vivian commented to his nephew that they had time to kill him before he got to Fort Garland.

Vivian then asked, "Did you see a woman about here?" Garcia denied that he had seen a woman, but unfortunately she lifted her head above the wagon box and was spotted by Vivian. Vivian commanded, "Put that prostitute of the American out of the wagon or we will fire on you."

Garcia refused, and the woman cried out, "Don Pedro, don't perish for me; they are Christians and won't hurt me." As she got out, Garcia drove off. Vivian Espinosa tied the woman hand and foot and raped her.

The man who had escaped managed to reach Fort Garland where he stated his case to the fort's commanding officer, Colonel Sam Tappan. Immediately, Tappan sent out soldiers to intercept Pedro Garcia and look for the woman. From Garcia they learned they were dealing with the notorious Espinosas. The soldiers found the woman and brought her back to the fort.

Colonel Tappan then sent for a scout named Tom Tobin. At the time, Tobin lived about six miles south of Fort Garland on Trinchera Creek. He raised cattle part of the year and spent the rest of his time with his Mexican wife and small daughter at Costilla, New Mexico, just south of the Colorado line.

Tom Tobin was a picturesque figure. He rode a black horse and wore a black hat, shirt, trousers, and boots. He kept two loaded revolvers in his gun belt, one on each side. Although illiterate, Tobin actively supported the local school system and even became president of the school board.

At Fort Garland, Tappan met with Tobin and offered a reward to bring in the heads of the Espinosas. Tobin wanted to hunt the murderers alone, but Tappan insisted that he take some soldiers with him.

On September 7, 1863, Tom Tobin, along with a Lieutenant Baldwin, fifteen soldiers, one civilian, and a Mexican boy, left the fort. On the first day out, Tobin located the Espinosas, but he lost them during a chase through heavy pine and quaking aspen. By tracking the murderers up a streambed, Tobin again got within sight of the killers as they disappeared over a ridge.

After camping in the mountains, Tobin, the Mexican boy, Lieutenant Baldwin, and a half-dozen soldiers rode down La Veta Creek. Tobin saw the tracks of two oxen and surmised that the Espinosas were driving them. He tracked them on foot through thick groves of pine and aspen and soon discovered they had let one of the oxen go. Tobin figured they were taking the other ox to their camp to be butchered. Baldwin was unable to follow with the horses and was instructed by Tobin to stay at a certain point and wait. The boy, two soldiers, and Tobin continued their hunt on foot.

In many places Tobin had to crawl under fallen timber to track the men. In the distance, he saw some crows circling overhead; he reasoned the birds must be circling over the butchering site. Tobin watched and moved carefully. Finally he saw the camp. He told the soldiers not to speak or make any noise.

As Tobin approached, he saw Vivian. The scout accidently stepped on a stick, and Vivian jumped for his gun. But before the murderer could get his gun, Tobin fired his muzzle-loading rifle, hitting Vivian in the side. Espinosa bellowed like a bull and cried out, "Jesus favor me," then yelled to his nephew, "Escape. I am killed."

Tobin saw the boy running out of a grove of aspens and ordered the soldiers to fire. All of the rounds missed. In the meantime, Tobin calmly tipped his powder horn to the muzzle of his rifle, dropped in a patch and a ball, and tamped it home. He capped the gun, raised it to his shoulder, and fired at the running boy. The ball broke the young Espinosa's back just above the hip, killing him instantly.

In the meantime, Vivian Espinosa crawled over to some fallen trees and braced himself with his revolver in hand. Tobin ran back to Vivian, keeping out of the line of fire. Vivian recognized Tobin and called out his name. A soldier began walking toward Vivian. The murderer fired, but the round missed. Tobin disarmed Vivian, took hold of his hair, and drew his head over a log. Using his hunting knife, Tobin cut off Espinosa's head. The Mexican boy was sent to cut off the head of the other Espinosa.

Tobin delivered the heads to Colonel Tappan in a gunny sack. However, it took several years for Tom Tobin to collect his reward of fifteen hundred dollars. Tobin did receive a

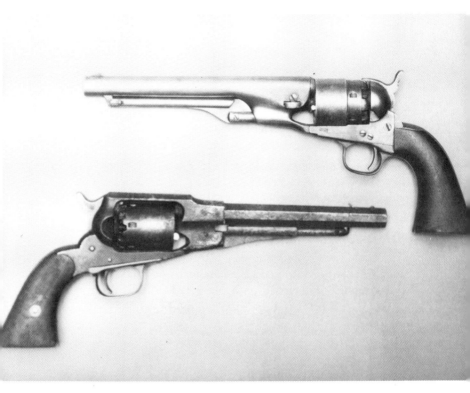

These are the revolvers Tom Tobin removed from the bodies of the Espinosas after he killed them. The upper revolver is an 1860 Colt Army, and the lower revolver is an 1858 Remington Army. *Colorado Historical Society*

beautiful silver inlaid rifle and two hundred dollars from a private citizen.

The hideous reign of terror by the Espinosas had come to an end. A diary found with their belongings claimed they had killed twenty-two Anglos.

Notes

1. It is believed that Governor John Evans offered a twenty-five hundred dollar reward for the Espinosas and advertised it in the *Rocky Mountain News*. After the Espinosas were killed by Tom Tobin, Evans denied that such a reward was ever offered. No evidence has ever come to the surface that shows conclusively that the reward was advertised.

References

Everett, George G. and Dr. Wendell F. Hutchinson. *Under the Angel of Shavano*. Denver: Golden Bell Press, 1963, pp. 387–390.

Hewett, Edgar L. "Tom Tobin." *Colorado Magazine* 23, no. 5 (September 1946): 210–211.

Keeton, Else. "The Story of Dead Man's Canyon and of the Espinosas." *Colorado Magazine* 8, no. 1 (January 1931): 34–38.

Kelsey, Harry E., Jr. *Frontier Capitalist*. Boulder: Pruett Publishing Co., 1969, pp. 133, 289.

Kildare, Maurice. "The Killers." *Great West* (1974): 20–25.

San Luis Valley Historical Society. *The San Luis Valley Historian* 13, no. 2. Alamosa, Colo. (1980): 2–3.

Simmons, Virginia McConnell. *Bayou Salado*. Colorado Springs: Century One Press, 1966, pp. 114–117.

——— . *The San Luis Valley*. Boulder: Pruett Publishing Co., 1979, pp. 79–80.

Tobin, Thomas T. "The Capture of the Espinosas." *Colorado Magazine* 9, no. 2 (March 1932): 59–66.

Mr. Berry, a resident of Hamilton in South Park, tracked the Reynolds gang like an Indian. He later rode to Denver to warn everyone and to try to raise a posse. *Drawing by B. D. Titsworth, permission granted by Kenneth Englert*

Confederate Guerrillas in Colorado

Jim Reynolds and his band of eight raiders were the only known Confederate guerrillas to "attack" Colorado Territory. Their plan was to plunder Colorado of its mined gold and silver and bring the loot back to finance the Confederacy.

The action began when the band approached South Park from Canon City on Sunday, July 24, 1864. The vast expanse of South Park was at its best with lush grass, plenty of water, and a backdrop of high, snow-capped peaks.

Reynolds and his guerrillas picked the Adolph Guirand ranch between Hartsel and Fairplay to spend the night. Guirand, a Frenchman by birth, proved to be a gracious host. He had no idea why these men were visiting him. He provided his visitors with supper, a place to sleep, and breakfast the next morning. The gang repaid his kindness by stealing his horses, robbing him of his cash, and molesting his wife.

A stranger who had also stayed the previous night at Guirand's ranch noticed the gang the following morning. He had heard tales of an approaching band of Confederate guerrillas and, without waiting for breakfast, rode off to Dan McLaughlin's stage station, which was about eight miles out of Fairplay on the road to Denver.

Shortly after the stranger left, the Reynolds gang saddled up and took off in the same direction. Before reaching Dan McLaughlin's stage stop, the gang encountered Major H. H. DeMary, manager of a local gold mine. The major was riding along the main road to Denver. He was known for keeping his gold in buckets, pails, boots, jars, cans, and so on. When the Reynolds gang shook the major down, all they got was a measly one hundred dollars.

As if to insult this dignified man, one of the gang members snatched the major's hat and placed his own shabby headgear on him. DeMary was a big man, weighing about 225 pounds,

Jim Reynolds and his band of eight raiders were the only known Confederates to "attack" Colorado. During a holdup, one of the gang members taunted Major H. H. DeMary. *Drawing by B. D. Titsworth, permission granted by Kenneth Englert*

and the hat didn't fit his large head. One of the gang members took hold of the brim with both hands and forced the hat down over the major's ears. "Damn you, wear that . . . it just fits you," he taunted.

Around eight o'clock that morning, the Reynolds gang arrived at Dan McLaughlin's stage station with their prisoner, Major DeMary. The stranger from the Guirand ranch was eating breakfast.

These heavily armed men created uneasiness at the station. When the stage arrived, the gang grabbed the lead horses. At gunpoint, they forced the driver, Abe Williamson, and the line's owner, Billy McClellan, off the stage. Fortunately, there were no passengers in the stage. McClellan was robbed of four hundred dollars, a fine gold watch, and his revolver. The guerrillas broke open the U.S. mail container, and the strongbox yielded around three thousand dollars. They also stole the horses, and since they had had their fun with him, they released Major DeMary.

A Mr. Berry, who lived in the nearby town of Hamilton, was in the stage station at the time. He talked to the stranger and learned of the gang's activity at the Guirand ranch. They watched as the gang chopped the spokes out of the coach wheels. Without being seen, Berry slipped off to warn the residents of Hamilton. He told the town's people what had happened, then galloped off on the road over Kenosha Pass to Denver to warn everyone along the line.

When he reached the main road, he discovered, much to his dismay, that the band was ahead of him. He tracked them, Indian style, keeping out of sight. At the Michigan House, the gang stole more horses. On top of Kenosha Pass at the Kenosha House, they robbed the proprietor, Mrs. Harriman. They admitted to her that they were rebel soldiers from the Confederacy. After they had eaten dinner, they returned all but two dollars to Mrs. Harriman.

Berry continued to track the guerrillas until they reached the Omaha House. This large, two-story building was about one-and-a-half miles southwest of present-day Conifer. Berry rode through the trees to the Junction House in an effort to get ahead of the gang. The Junction House was located about a mile north of Conifer, at the point where the road to Evergreen met the road to Denver.

Berry tried to raise an impromptu posse. He found some weapons at the house but couldn't motivate anyone to stand up and fight. Maybe they simply didn't believe him. In any event he went to bed disgusted, and the Reynolds gang stayed at the Omaha House for the night.

On Tuesday morning, July 26, Berry was again eager to start out after the Reynolds gang. He did get one man, Charles Hall, to follow him. But as soon as the two men arrived at the Omaha House, they were captured. The robbers snatched Hall's pistol and removed his necktie pin. They returned the pin later because of Hall's pleading that it was a gift from a friend.

The gang members were jovial and talked freely about how they had come to Colorado to plunder the countryside and planned to return with money for the Confederacy. They also mentioned that they would be met by a larger party at the base of the mountains.

James Reynolds asked Berry, "Is there much to get to Denver?" It's hard to believe he missed seeing Berry at Dan McLaughlin's stage station, so his question may have been meant simply to taunt Berry.

Berry replied, "No! I've just come from Denver and it's devilish dull there. You can't get anything worth going after."

"Did you know that the coach from Montgomery won't be down at the usual time?" continued Reynolds.

Berry acted surprised, exclaiming, "For God's sake, why?"

"Our company is running the road now," boasted Reynolds, "and we have changed the time." As if to prove his point, he drew a few letters he had taken from the U.S. mail out of his pocket. He handed one over to Berry saying, "Here is one of Uncle Sam's mail." When Berry asked if any of the letters were for him, the outlaws burst out laughing.

Reynolds released Hall and Berry since the outlaws believed the men could do them little harm. As soon as Hall and Berry were out of sight, the two rode hard for the Junction House by cutting through the trees. Berry continued on toward Denver, warning residents along the way. He galloped down the road much like Paul Revere, changing horses as often as possible. He advised the ranchers along the way to drive their livestock away from the road. He galloped through the streets of Denver and right up to the offices of the *Rocky Mountain News*.

It was a couple of hours before the gang reached the Junction House. They hid in the forest and watched the house, then when they were sure the law wasn't around, they stole fresh horses. The rebels pumped the proprietor and his guests for information, asking where the money was kept in Denver. That evening they rode back to the Omaha House to spend another night.

The next morning, Reynolds and his gang started up the road toward Shaffer's Crossing. In the meantime, Major DeMary had organized a posse of about thirty men from South Park. As the posse came down the main road, the rebels spotted it and escaped up Deer Creek.

Berry had done his job of alerting residents of Denver, but it took more than a day before a cavalry unit, under the command of Captain Maynard, could leave Denver. The cavalry rode to the Omaha House only to find the Reynolds gang was long gone.

Thursday, July 29, was an uneventful day for all concerned. The posse from South Park made its way back to Harriman's at Kenosha Pass and searched the area for the rebels. The cavalry traveled up the main wagon road over the pass and reached the Kenosha House the following day.

On July 30, the rebels ate breakfast at Slaght's freight station, about a quarter of a mile from Shawnee. Here they learned that a posse was after them.

One of the Denver soldiers had fallen behind his unit and reached the freight station at the same time as the rebels. He managed to keep out of sight and escape through a back window. He rode hard for the Kenosha House, where he alerted his unit. The cavalry made a mad dash down the road, only to find the rebels gone once again. They then gave up and returned to Denver.

In the meantime, a man named Jack Sparks rounded up a dozen posse members from the Swan and Snake rivers area near Breckenridge. They rode along the Snake River past Keystone, over the Continental Divide, and down the North Fork of the South Platte river. Late Saturday, they sighted a campfire near Harriman's Kenosha House. They left their horses and crept down toward the fire until they were within seventy-five yards or so. The posse knew that the men were members of the Reynolds gang. The rebels heard noises in the dark perimeter

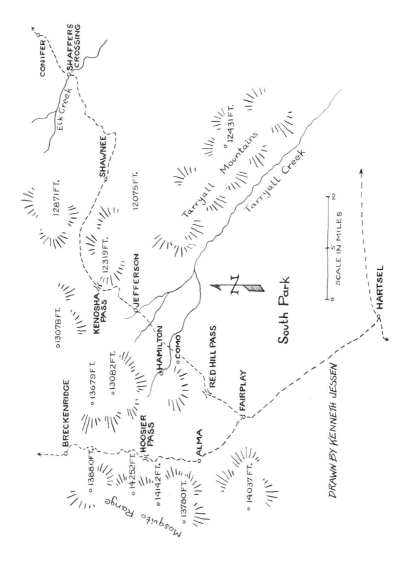

CONIFER

SHAFFERS CROSSING

Elk Creek

SHAWNEE

12871 FT.

12075 FT.

Tarryall Mountains

12431 FT.

Tarryall Creek

13078 FT.

12319 FT.

KENOSHA PASS

JEFFERSON

N

South Park

SCALE IN MILES

HARTSEL

13679 FT.

13082 FT.

HAMILTON

COMO

RED HILL PASS

FAIRPLAY

BRECKENRIDGE

HOOSIER PASS

ALMA

13880 FT.

14252 FT.

14142 FT.

13780 FT.

14037 FT.

Mosquito Range

DRAWN BY KENNETH JESSEN

around the fire and grabbed their guns. As they ran for cover, Sparks told them to stop. This order was followed by a volley of shots delivered by the posse. It was too dark to continue the chase, and the posse retreated to the Kenosha House for the night.

The next morning, July 31, the posse rode back to the campsite and found one dead rebel. He had been shot through the breast. No trace could be found of any of the other men. The dead man was identified as Owen Singleterry, and he had on the blue coat of a Union soldier. All of the belongings of the rebels were found at the campsite except the things they had managed to carry off during the night. Among the many items left were coats, two revolvers, one shotgun, three saddle bags, four muskets, and one spy glass. Some cash was found, along with a package of amalgam gold taken from the stagecoach, and a number of letters were recovered. It appeared that the gang had escaped into the night with very little of their plunder.

Dr. Cooper, a member of the posse, cut off Singleterry's head and took it into Fairplay. This grizzly reminder of the Reynold's gang was preserved in alcohol and remained in Fairplay for a number of years.

The attack by the posse broke up the rebels. One of the gang members, Tom Holliman, headed toward Canon City. On August 1, he was captured at a ranch house where he had stopped to rest. Evidently expecting to be shot on sight, he fainted. He was revived and, to save his skin, agreed to tell all he knew about his comrades.

The following day, returning to the scene of one of their crimes, four rebels came back to Adolph Guiraud's ranch. The Guirauds were in Denver, and the gang stole some provisions. They headed toward Fairplay and forced the occupants of an isolated house to fix them some food.

As word about the rebels spread, more South Park residents got into the posse business. On August 9, at least seventy-five left Fairplay to find the guerrillas. At the head of the group rode Tom Holliman. He was forced to ride in leg irons. The posse continued to chase the rebels for several days until the four men were captured. They were taken to Denver and received a military trial. Reynolds and two others made it into New Mexico and escaped.

The five prisoners were turned over to Company A, 3rd Regiment of the Colorado Cavalry, to be taken to Fort Lyon. En route, at a place called California Ranch near the Russeville site on Upper Cherry Creek, the prisoners were shot to death under mysterious circumstances. It was later reported that three skeletons were found at this site, lashed to trees with bullet holes in their skulls. No remains of the other two prisoners were found.

References

Collier, William Ross and Edwin Victor Westrate. *Dave Cook of the Rockies*. New York: Rufus Rockwell Wilson, 1936, p. 48.

Drago, Harry Sinclair. *Lost Bonanzas*. New York: Dodd, Mead & Co., 1966, pp. 132–143.

Englert, Kenneth. "Raids by Reynolds." In *1956 Brand Book*, Denver: The Westerners, 1957, pp. 151–173.

Hall, Frank. *History of the State of Colorado*. Chicago: The Blakely Printing Co., 1889, pp. 313–317.

Perkin, Robert L. *The First Hundred Years*. New York: Doubleday & Co., 1959, pp. 250–251.

Shaw, Dorothy Price. "The Cragin Collection." *Colorado Magazine* 25, no. 4 (May 1948): 177–178.

Simmons, Virginia McConnell. *Bayou Salado*. Colorado Springs: Century One Press, 1966, pp. 117–119.

Saloon owner Dan Hill was accidentally shot to death in a gunfight involving the outlaw Sanford Duggan. The event happened the evening of November 23, 1868, in Golden during an attempt to arrest two members of the Musgrove gang. *From Cook,* Hands Up!, *1897 ed.*

The End of the Musgrove Gang

B y the summer of 1868, a gang of robbers and horse thieves had firmly established itself at Bonner Springs in Larimer County. At the springs was a natural fort created by the surrounding rock formation, and L. H. Musgrove and his gang operated from this location. They stole horses, mules, and cattle throughout northern Colorado and southern Wyoming. Their primary targets were government animals. A pair of good mules could bring $350 to $700 at a time when wages rarely exceeded $2 a day.

The Indians were often blamed for horse theft, which formed a perfect cover for the Musgrove gang. During September 1864, a herd of fifty cattle at Fort Fred Steele in Wyoming was stolen during the night. The soldiers made every effort to track the rustlers and recover the cattle, but Musgrove was just too clever. During October, all of the cavalry horses at the fort were stolen. Some of the soldiers on guard that night were thought to have been in on the operation, since they disappeared with the horses. Again, a company of soldiers was sent out after the thieves, but to no avail.

The raids continued. The thieves became bold and cut open the quartermaster's tent and removed the safe. The safe was hauled to a gulch and blown open. Musgrove and his gang got away with eighteen hundred dollars.

Abner Loomis, a prominent Fort Collins citizen, knew Musgrove and knew of his activities. Loomis sold vegetables to him from his farm in Pleasant Valley along the Cache la Poudre River. Loomis warned the outlaw that if he ever stole a horse or mule belonging to any settler in the area he, Loomis, would personally organize a posse. He said he would hunt Musgrove down and hang him on the spot. Because Musgrove needed a supply point, he did not bother any of the residents of Pleasant Valley.

Nevertheless, in the fall of 1868 Loomis learned that Musgrove had a price on his head and elected to try to capture him. During the closing days of October, he rode out to where he knew he could find the gang. Loomis was unarmed, and as he approached the camp, Musgrove, with a gun in hand, asked him to halt. Loomis told Musgrove he was on a peaceful mission, and he was allowed to pass into the camp.

Loomis played upon the gang leader's greed by telling him about a fine horse a short distance away just ripe for the taking. Musgrove now believed Loomis to be an ally and rode off with him to get the horse. Abner invited the outlaw to have a bit to eat first at his home in Pleasant Valley. As they were eating, Marshal Haskell from Denver entered the room with a gun in his hand. Musgrove could do nothing but give up. It was a setup; Haskell had been hiding near the home, waiting for the men to show up.[1] The outlaw was taken to Denver and placed in the jail on Larimer Street.

L. H. Musgrove was a large man and had steady nerves. Originally from Mississippi, he was a born leader. He was attracted to California by the gold rush and settled in Napa Valley. During the Civil War, he quarreled with another man over the conflict and shot the other party in cold blood. This forced him to leave Napa Valley. Next, he killed two men in Nevada and moved on to become an Indian trader at Fort Halleck, Wyoming. His stay there lasted until a half-breed called him a liar. Musgrove calmly drew his revolver, took aim, and planted a bullet squarely into the man's forehead.

It was after this last incident that he organized a network of horse thieves. Musgrove had operators to unload the stolen animals in a number of western states. The gang would steal from one area, drive the stock hundreds of miles, then sell it, only to steal again. Sometimes they stole stock from the very person that purchased stolen stock.

After Musgrove was brought to Denver and placed in jail, as many as twenty outlaws headed into the Queen City to free their leader. The group was led by Edward "Heartless" Franklin and Sanford Duggan. Franklin's list of accomplishments included stealing mules from Fort Saunders, Wyoming. One day he drove some government mules several miles out on the plains with seventeen soldiers in hot pursuit. Just as he was about to be captured, he dismounted and pushed up a pile of sand. He hid behind the pile, and the soldiers opened fire. A gun battle raged for more than an hour. Finally, a lucky shot struck Franklin in the breast. He was taken to Fort Saunders, where he recovered from his wound. Once he was strong enough, he escaped from the fort.

Heartless Edward Franklin eventually became a member of the Musgrove gang. Franklin was quite faithful to his leader, and the two lived through many close calls. They had vowed eternally to protect each other at all cost.

In 1861, when he was sixteen, Sanford Duggan came to Colorado from Pennsylvania, and at eighteen, he shot down a man in Black Hawk. For this, Duggan spent a short time in prison, then escaped. In Denver, he became friends with a prostitute named Kittie Wells who sold herself to support both of them. One night Duggan pistol-whipped her almost to death and was arrested. Next, he appeared in Laramie as its city marshal. This job lasted until Laramie's citizens discovered his true character and ran him out of town. Duggan eventually joined the Musgrove gang also.

Franklin and Duggan came to Denver to rescue Musgrove, but before they could do so, the pair perpetrated a series of crimes that distracted them from their original purpose. They met James Torrence on Blake Street and robbed him of twenty-two dollars. Alex Delap was their next intended victim, but he wisely left his valuables at home. On Lawrence Street, the pair discovered the Honorable Orson Brooks, a justice of the peace and police magistrate. Franklin and Duggan had no idea who he was. Brooks was on his way home, and the two followed him to a deserted place. The judge was robbed of $135, but he could have been killed, for it was Brooks who had presided over the trial of Duggan for his assault on Kittie Wells. The judge immediately recognized Duggan, and the latter thought he knew the judge. Duggan remarked to his partner, "Let's plant the damn old snoozer—what d'you say?"

Franklin agreed. The judge, however, convinced the men they had been mistaken about his identity. After treating him to a liberal dose of profanity, the two scoundrels let him go.

The citizens of Denver were indignant over the robbery of their esteemed citizen. The case was placed in the hands of the capable General David Cook who, at the time, was town marshal and the head of the Rocky Mountain Detective Agency.

Cook received a valuable clue from Judge Brooks. One of his bills was a twenty that had been torn and was repaired with a piece of official paper from his office. All of the officers in Denver and the surrounding towns were asked to pass the word and look for the unique bill.

On Sunday, November 23, 1868, just two days after the robbery, the two men passed the telltale twenty during a drunken binge in Golden. It was dusk before Marshal Cook and his men were ready to ride the eight miles from Denver up Clear Creek to Golden. At nine o'clock, they entered town and quickly learned from Sheriff Keith just where the men were.

Franklin had been drinking heavily and was sleeping it off at the Overland House. Duggan, on the other hand, was still at it in Dan Hill's saloon. The company of seven law officers headed toward the saloon. In the dark street they overhead two men remark, "What do these sons of bitches of officers want. That's Dave Cook from Denver." Sheriff Keith whispered to Cook that one of the men was Duggan, and the other was saloon owner Dan Hill.

Hill and Duggan walked across a vacant lot and entered the rear door of Hill's saloon. Duggan had apparently left his revolver there. Cook directed Keith and the other men to guard the front while he and one other man approached the rear of the saloon.

The saloon was totally dark. Cook and his men noticed the glow of a cigar as they approached. The rear door was open, and a man with a gun appeared. He handed the gun to the man smoking the cigar. It was too dark to distinguish their faces, but when the man with the cigar got hold of the pistol he fired immediately. A bit of Cook's blue soldier's overcoat was nipped by the ball. Now the officers knew it was Duggan who had fired. Duggan sent another round at the officers. Cook returned the fire and told his partner to do likewise. One of the men in the saloon fell to the ground, and the other ran off into the darkness.

It was Duggan who escaped, and he fired at the officers as he ran. The man they had shot was Dan Hill. He was hit in the left side of the abdomen, and the ball nearly passed through his body. He was a good fellow and well liked by the community. Hill died twelve hours later. Cook was criticized for firing too quickly and killing an innocent man.

With blood running down his head and thrashing around like a wild animal, Edward Franklin was shot to death by detectives General David Cook and Frank Smith in a Golden hotel. *From Cook,* Hands Up!, *1897 ed.*

Now it was Franklin's turn. The posse headed toward the Overland House, and upon their arrival, they asked the proprietor which room was occupied by Franklin. The officers entered the unlocked room quietly, with Sheriff Keith carrying a candle. Sure enough, the man stretched out in the bed was Franklin. The scar from the gunshot wound he had received near Fort Saunders was visible. As he rolled over, his eyes opened. Cook laid a hand on him saying, "Franklin, we want you."

"The hell you do!" was his response.

"Yes, come on quietly."

Franklin exploded, "Quietly be damned! Where's my gun? No damn officer from Denver can arrest me. I'm not that sort of stuff. You can make up your mind to that." Franklin rose to his knees, striking out at the officers with his fists. This caused the men to back away from the bed. Cook produced his handcuffs and approached Franklin.

"Oh, it's irons you have, is it?" Franklin lunged at the officers and exclaimed, "If that's what you're up to, I have some myself." He reached for the cocked revolver he kept under his pillow. Quickly, one of the posse members struck Franklin a solid blow over the head with the barrel of his revolver. With blood running down his head, Franklin thrashed around like a wild animal, yelling, "Come on all of you!"

He got to his feet and defied the men to shoot him. "If you want to shoot, put to there—there!" Franklin shouted, slapping his hand several times against his chest. He continued to act like a madman while the officers showed considerable restraint. He vowed to die before being arrested.

Franklin made a desperate lunge for a revolver that Cook had placed on a table. Cook and one of the other officers, Frank Smith, fired almost simultaneously. Franklin tumbled over on the bloodstained bed from the impact of two balls that passed through his heart an inch apart. He was now a dead, harmless man. The proprietor of the Overland House was paid $50 to cover the damage to the bed.

The officers returned to their Denver homes near dawn. They slept until late morning, exhausted from their experiences in Golden. In the meantime, Musgrove was boasting from his cell that his friends were planning his escape and the law would be powerless to prevent it. Denver citizens agreed that something needed to be done to discourage any attempt by Musgrove's friends to spring the outlaw.

The suggestion came up to lynch Musgrove. The idea spread like a prairie fire, and by three o'clock in the afternoon, Monday, November 24, hundreds of men were moved into action. They marched down Larimer Street toward the jail. The members of the mob made no effort to hide their identity. Observers noticed doctors, lawyers, and other prominent citizens. The mob continued to grow and came to a halt in front of the jail. Someone shouted, "Shall Musgrove be taken out of jail?"

The crowd responded, "Yes."

The same individual asked, "Shall he be hanged when taken out?"

Again, a resounding "yes" came from the crowd.

Members of the lynch mob entered the jail and met with no resistance. From his cell, Musgrove had overheard what was going on out in the street. He said, "Come on! I am ready for you."

He was armed with a heavy pine knot, which he swung at anyone who attempted to enter his cell. Several shots were fired over his head. Musgrove surrendered and was pushed toward the Larimer Street bridge over Cherry Creek. He was sullen and glanced around, hoping some of his gang would show up and perform a last minute rescue. At the bridge he asked for a paper and a pencil to write to his wife and one of his friends. Bending over the railing at the center of the bridge, he scratched out two notes. He wrote, with a steady hand, the following note to his wife:[2]

> My dear wife—Before this reaches you I will bee no more. Mary I am as you know innocent of the charges made against me. I do not know that they are agoing to me for unless it is because I am acquainted with Ed Franklin—godd will protect you I hope. Good by for ever as ever yours. Sell what I have and keep it.
> L. H. Musgrove

As he wrote, his legs were tied. He was told to get into a wagon. The wagon was driven down the bank and under the bridge. Below the middle span a noose was dangling. He was

On the afternoon of November 24, 1868, a Denver lynch mob removed L. H. Musgrove from his cell and hung him at the Larimer Street bridge over Cherry Creek. During the process, Musgrove coolly removed a piece of cigarette paper from his vest pocket and fumbled for some shreds of tobacco. He rolled a cigarette, keeping his composure until the last. *From Cook,* Hands Up!, *1897 ed.*

given the opportunity to prepare for his end. He remarked, "Go on with your work."

He was ordered to stand on the wagon seat as the rope was tied around his neck. A citizen named Captain Scudder began addressing the crowd from the bridge about how illegal their proceedings were. Musgrove remained sullen and calm. He coolly removed a piece of cigarette paper from his vest pocket and fumbled in the other pocket for some shreds of tobacco. He rolled a cigarette, keeping his composure. The captain continued to talk while Musgrove smoked his last cigarette.

Musgrove's hat was pulled over his eyes and the order was given to the driver to move the wagon. Musgrove was taunted by the crowd, which asked where his gang was in his time of need. He leaped into the air, hoping to make his final moments quick ones, but landed in the wagon bed. He made a second leap, and this time the wagon had moved out of the way. Musgrove's weight came down on the rope, breaking his neck, and death came instantly. The hat was pulled from the dead man's head, revealing the same sullen expression, void of fear, that he had worn throughout the lynching.

A man that appeared to be the leader of the lynch mob addressed the crowd, telling them that a dozen or so men just like Musgrove still remained in Denver. He then threatened to hang any of them after twenty-four hours. Before the next afternoon, as so aptly put by Jerome Smiley in *the History of Denver*, "some forty or fifty individuals, each of whom was conscious that his record entitled him to a place in the speaker's list of a dozen, were putting stretches of the plains between themselves and Denver as fast as they could."

Duggan was arrested in Cheyenne and brought back to Denver. Law officers did what they could to prevent a second lynching, but his neck was stretched also, this time from a cottonwood tree along Cherry Street.

Sanford Duggan was lynched from a cottonwood tree along Cherry Creek in Denver on December 2, 1868. Photographers fought over the right to obtain exclusive photographs of this gruesome scene. *Colorado Historical Society*

Notes

1. The account given here comes from the *History of Larimer County*. It differs from the one in *Hands Up!*, which is an account of the reminiscences of General D. J. Cook, superintendent of the Rocky Mountain Detective Agency. According to *Hands Up!*, Musgrove was cornered in Colorado after he had taken shelter near the Cache la Poudre River. The outlaw raised a white flag and told the posse to pick out the stolen stock, but he was too well barricaded to be captured there, and was able to escape to Wyoming, where he was finally captured.

2. This letter was saved by General Cook and reproduced in *Hands Up!*

References

[Dawson, Thomas Fulton?] *Hands Up! or Twenty Years of Detective Life in the Mountains and on the Plains.* Denver: W. F. Robinson Printing Co, 1882. Reprint. Norman, Okla: University of Oklahoma Press, 1958, pp. 39–65.

Smiley, Jerome C., ed. *History of Denver.* Denver: Old American Publishing Co., 1901, p. 437.

Watrous, Ansel. *History of Larimer County.* Fort Collins: Courier Printing and Publishing Co., 1911, pp. 104–105.

Griff Evans looks pretty harmless with his dog "Murphy." Evans, however, gunned down Rocky Mountain Jim in Estes Park during the spring of 1874. *Estes Park Area Museum*

Rocky Mountain Jim Murdered in Estes Park

James Nugent, known as Rocky Mountain Jim, was a true character of the Old West. He was excellent at spinning yarns, and he made lasting romantic impressions on the women he met. He was a poet, a mountain man, a drunkard, and a liar.

No one really knows where he was born. Jim described himself as being the nephew of a General Beauregard and as hailing from the South. He also told others that he was the son of a British army officer stationed in Montreal, Canada. He claimed to have worked for the Hudson's Bay Company and the American Fur Company. He reported that he had homesteaded in Missouri and fought with Quantrell. He was said to be a defrocked priest or a former schoolmaster. Records of births, marriages, and deaths in Montreal yield no mention of a Nugent family. The Hudson's Bay Company's library and records fail to uncover any reference to James Nugent. State historical societies in places where he said he had lived turned up nothing. His past is truly a mystery.

During July 1871, Rocky Mountain Jim was making his way up the Grand (Colorado) River to Grand Lake. He left his camp to visit a deerlick nearby, taking his knife and a revolver but leaving his rifle behind. As he came upon several deer, his dog ran howling out of the nearby bushes. The dog was followed by a large cinnamon bear with her two cubs. The dog ran right to Jim, and so did the bear.

Jim knew he was in serious trouble and began firing his revolver at the approaching bear, hitting her four times. The mother bear bit into Jim's left arm at the elbow, crushing it, then hurled him to the ground. Jim placed the pistol against the bear's body and fired a fifth shot. The bear released his arm and bit him in the head, ripping Jim's scalp to the bone. Jim collapsed into unconsciousness.

When he revived, Rocky Mountain Jim found himself alone in a pool of his own blood. His clothes were ripped to shreds, and deep wounds scarred his body. His right eye was hidden under the torn scalp, and his left thumb was missing. Using his one good arm, he managed to mount his trusty mule and headed for Grand Lake. He fell from the animal several times during the tip.

Two men living at Grand Lake were the first to see Jim. One of them thought he had been scalped by Indians. The men tended his wounds, then one left to find a doctor. About fifteen miles away, a doctor was found who returned to the cabin to help.

By August, Rocky Mountain Jim had recovered sufficiently to leave Grand Lake. A carbuncle about the size of a hen's egg covered his right eye. The right side of his face was badly disfigured. The bear's paw had almost surgically sliced across the eyelid, closing the eye.

Rocky Mountain Jim constructed a crude cabin on the trail into Estes Park at the head of Muggins Gulch. There, he raised cattle and did some trapping. Below Jim's cabin lived Griffith Evans in an old cabin built by Joel Estes, the park's first settler. Evans was a small man of Welsh descent, and he and Jim got along quite well during those early days of settlement in Estes Park. But things changed as more visitors and settlers came into the area. It was not long before Griff Evans realized that he could make a better living providing food and lodging to visitors than he could by ranching. Jim, on the other hand, was a born hunter and could not reconcile himself to change.

As early as 1871, Griff Evans planned to build an informal hotel for visitors to the park. Estes Park was becoming known as a haven for restoring one's health, hunting, fishing, and enjoying the magnificent scenery. Evans began constructing cabins around the small lake formed by a low dam on Fish Creek. His wife cooked meals for visitors, and a week's board and lodging came to eight dollars.

One of the first visitors to take advantage of this pioneer dude ranch was Isabella L. Bird, a well-known English author.

Rocky Mountain Jim was the first person she met in Estes Park. As her horse passed Jim's cabin at the head of Muggins Gulch, the barking of Jim's dog brought him to the door. Miss

Bird wrote in her book, *A Lady's Life in the Rocky Mountains,* the following description of Jim Nugent and his cabin:

> Among the scrub, not far from the track, was a rude, black log cabin . . . with smoke coming out of the roof and window . . . it looked like the den of a wild beast. The mud roof was covered with lynx, beaver, and other furs laid out to dry, beaver paws were pinned out on the logs, a part of a carcass of a deer hung at one end of the cabin, a skinned beaver lay in front of a heap of peltry just within the door, and antlers of deer and old horse-shoes, and offal of many animals lay about the den. Roused by the growling of the dog, his owner came out, a broad, thick-set man about middle height, with an old cap on his head, and wearing a grey hunting suit almost falling to pieces, a digger's scarf knotted about his waist, a knife in his belt and a revolver sticking out of the breast pocket of his coat. The marvel was how his clothes hung together, and on him. His face was remarkable. He is a man about forty-five, and must have been strikingly handsome. He has large gray-blue eyes [sic], deeply set, a handsome aquiline nose, and a very handsome mouth. His face was smooth shaven except for a dense mustache and imperial. Tawny hair in thin, uncared-for curls, fell from under his hunter's cap and over his collar. One eye was entirely gone, and the loss made one side of his face repulsive, while the other might have been modeled in marble. In a cultured tone of voice he asked if there were anything he could do for me? I asked for some water, and he brought some in a battered tin, gracefully apologizing for not having anything more presentable. He was a true child of nature.

Another British subject who encountered Rocky Mountain Jim was Lord Dunraven, a wealthy earl who enjoyed big-game hunting. He had heard of exceptional hunting in Estes Park, and in 1872 he came to investigate. Griffith Evans welcomed the earl and his hunting companions. Despite the fact that it was December and the temperature was below zero, Lord Dunraven immediately went in search of wild game. He found the hunting so good that he decided to buy the park as a private game preserve.

During Lord Dunraven's attempt to monopolize Estes Park, an Englishman named Hague was hired to start the process of securing land in the park. Hague decided he would like some female companionship while he was there. He had previously

Isabella L. Bird provided a detailed description of Rocky Mountain Jim in her book, *A Lady's Life in the Rocky Mountains*. *Estes Park Area Museum*

met a girl in Denver and later hired Rocky Mountain Jim to ride down and fetch her. He gave Jim a hundred dollars for expenses and as a commission for this errand. A week or so later, Jim returned empty handed. He told Hague that the woman refused to go up the park "and spend the summer with the . . . English dog for all the money he had." This angered Hague so much that he called Jim a thief, a liar, and a few other things. Using the muzzle of his cocked rifle, Jim poked Hague off his horse and forced the Englishman to retract what he had said.

The next day, June 19, 1874, Rocky Mountain Jim and his friend William Brown were headed for Muggins Gulch. The two men paused at Fish Creek to let their horses drink near the small cabin occupied by Hague. They started to move away about the time Hague and Griff Evans appeared at the cabin door. Evans had a double-barreled shotgun in his hands, and Hague urged him to use it on Jim, claiming that Jim had come to murder him.

Accounts differ as to the details of what took place next, but in any event, Evans discharged both barrels, first killing Jim's horse, then mortally wounding Jim. The attack took Jim by surprise, and he was unable to draw either his pistol or rifle.

A doctor out hunting in the area may have been drawn by the shots. When he arrived on the scene, he found five bullet wounds in Jim's head and face. One of the pieces of shot had penetrated the brain, but Jim was still conscious. Another piece of shot had gone through Jim's nose, splintering the bone. An attempt was made to move Jim to Evans's cabin, but Jim refused and requested he be taken back to his own home.

Immediately after the shooting, Evans raced to Fort Collins and secured a warrant for Jim's arrest on the grounds that Jim had threatened his life.

After Jim was carried back to his own cabin, the doctor reported that the wounded man would not live much longer. After several weeks, Rocky Mountain Jim was taken to Fort Collins where he filed charges, and warrants were sworn out for the arrest of Hague and Evans.

Jim was lodged at the Collins House. He was delirious at times, and he hovered between life and death until he died that September. Before he died, he wrote a detailed account of the shooting for the Fort Collins *Standard*.

Evans and Hague were tried before Rocky Mountain Jim's death. Hague was charged as an accessory in the shooting. The only grounds for the charge, however, was the comment he made to Evans after the latter had fired the first shot: "Give him the other barrel!" The court was told that Jim had threatened Hague several times with a loaded gun. The judge believed the story and felt that Hague was justified in making the comment.

As so well put by Rocky Mountain Jim Nugent in his statement to the press just before the trial, "Evans is turned loose to hunt up bail . . . or jump the country, as he sees fit. Haigh [sic] is as free as the wind, neither one of them are on a dollar of bonds." Jim went on to accuse Colorado of having a poor system of justice.

Possibly due to lack of evidence, Griffith Evans was found not guilty. William Brown, who was with Jim at the time of the shooting, checked into the Collins House to see Jim and to be a trial witness. Brown then vanished before the trial began, and there was speculation that he had been paid off by one of Lord Dunraven's men.

Rocky Mountain Jim left a will, but he had run up so many debts that there was nothing left for the beneficiaries.

References

Bancroft, Caroline. *Estes Park and Trail Ridge*. Boulder: Johnson Publishing Co., 1968, pp. 16-26.

Bird, Isabella L. *A Lady's Life in the Rocky Mountains*. Norman, Okla.: University of Oklahoma Press, 1960, pp. 78-101.

Buckholtz, C. W. *Rocky Mountain National Park*. Boulder: Colorado Associated University Press, 1983, pp. 69-71, 74-76.

Carothers, June E. *Estes Park: Past and Present*. Denver: The University of Denver Press, 1951, pp. 24-32.

Hicks, Dave. *Estes Park—From the Beginning*. Denver: Eagan Printing Co., 1976, pp. 19-33.

Mills, Enos A. *Early Estes Park*. Denver, 1911. Reprint. New York: Doubleday, Page & Co., 1972, pp. 32-38.

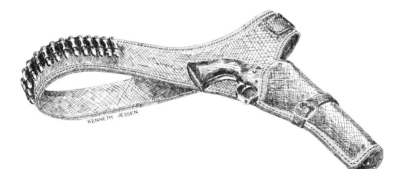

The Lake
County War

In 1874, in a secluded part of Colorado, there was an outbreak of mob violence unequaled in the state's early history for its impact on society. For a while, it destroyed any semblance of an organized judicial system. The situation was precipitated by a feud between two individuals and culminated in the murder of Judge E. F. Dyer. Known as the Lake County War, it was an example of the prevailing attitude toward frontier justice during the late 1800s. The end result was that Coloradoans came to understand the need for a stronger judicial system.

Below Twin Lakes, along the Arkansas River, was good ranch land. Abundant water from the small streams flowing out of the mountains combined with fertile land. Prior to 1879, the area was part of Lake County, but possibly because of the feud that developed, it was destined to become part of Chaffee County. During the early settlement days, activity in the area centered around mining. Ranching, however, grew in importance because of the need for horses, mules, and fodder. It was a rough life in this untamed region of Colorado, and it took individuals every bit as determined as the miners and prospectors to survive. Few settlers professed any goals but to take the world as it came. Most got along fairly peacefully, but occasionally claim jumping, land fraud, or arguments over irrigation water occurred. Resources were scarce, and competition for these resources was not governed by any formal law. The older settlers in the region tried to dominate newcomers. If the new settlers submitted, fine; if not, then means were applied to subdue their high spirits.

Elijah Gibbs was a newcomer, a straightforward man who moved into Lake County and lived next to George Harrington. When Gibbs tied his team near the place where a group of men was threshing, he was astonished to see his team moved and hitched to the machine without his permission. Gibbs became indignant over such rude treatment and ordered his team returned. This led to bad blood between the earlier settlers and himself.

On July 17, 1874, Gibbs fired his gun at George Harrington during a quarrel over their joint ownership of a ditch. Gibbs claimed the shot was an accident, and as Gibbs was a crack shot, this was probably true. That day, Gibbs was taken before the justice of the peace, then was allowed to return home, a decision that angered area residents. To make matters worse, the justice of the peace happened to be his brother-in-law.

That night, someone set fire to Harrington's outhouse. He got out of bed and ran out to extinguish the fire, using buckets of water from his well. He was shot in the back and died immediately. The circumstances made Gibbs the prime suspect.

Gibbs was arrested and taken to the town of Granite. Here he was to have stood trial, but he managed to obtained a change of venue to Denver. In Denver Gibbs was acquitted, which further angered the people of Lake County.

Elijah Gibbs returned to his Lake County home, intending to live down the suspicion that surrounded him. The older settlers would not leave the matter alone, however. A party of fifteen men gathered to take care of Gibbs. After filling themselves with liquor, they marched to his cabin and ordered him to come out and be hung like a man. Gibbs was with his pregnant wife and little child. Also inside the cabin was a neighbor and her child.

With a great deal of courage, Gibbs barred the door and prepared himself for the worst. The lynch mob piled brush against the back of the house and set it on fire. Gibbs put out the fire and dimmed the lights in the cabin. Using Gibbs's favorite racehorse as a shield, the mob was able to move more combustible material against the door.[1] Looking through a hole at the side of the door, Gibbs realized he and his family were in grave danger. When one of his assailants struck a match to set the pile on fire, Gibbs began shooting with his revolver. Sam and David Boon were mortally wounded, and their uncle, Finley Kane, died of a gunshot wound sometime later.[2]

Gibbs then discovered a man at the back of his cabin, climbing over the fence. He shot at the intruder through the window and wounded the man in the hip. The lynch mob scattered, and Gibbs quickly took his family to his brother-in-law's home below his own cabin.

The gun battle created a great deal of excitement, and friends of Gibbs suggested he leave the area for a while. With three of his friends, he began the trip through the mountains. He was pursued by members of the mob and was forced to ride cross-country. He finally managed to make it to Denver.

In early February 1875, the sheriff of Lake County, John Weldon, was sent to Denver with warrants to arrest Elijah Gibbs and the others who helped him escape. The sheriff made it clear that seventy men would be waiting for their return to Lake County. He also openly expressed his hostility toward Gibbs. Denver newspapers quickly picked up the story and pointed out that if Gibbs and his friends returned home they would be lynched on the spot.

When Sheriff Weldon arrived in Denver, he was arrested for drunkenness, a somewhat ludicrous charge in the hard-drinking early days of that town. After being disarmed, he was given the choice of going to his hotel or to jail to sober up. The way he was treated in Denver was quite insulting, and Weldon returned home empty-handed. This prompted Gibbs's enemies to form the "Committee of Safety."

The Committee of Safety grew in number to around sixty men. They made their headquarters at Nathrop's mill and rounded up individuals who might lean toward Gibbs's side of the incident involving the death of Harrington. The "suspects" were questioned as to their opinion of the incident. All roads into the southern end of Lake County were guarded, and no one was allowed to pass without permission of the committee.

Among the men brought in for questioning was Probate Judge Elias F. Dyer, son of the famous "snowshoe itinerant," Rev. John L. Dyer. They confined Judge Dyer in a schoolhouse with about thirty others, including a few children. The Committee of Safety, giving credence to no legal system but their own, charged Dyer with believing Gibbs to be innocent of the murder of Harrington, of giving false testimony at the Gibbs trial in Denver, of being pompous, and of proclaiming at the trial he was a probate judge.

A notice was signed by the committee and presented to Judge Dyer demanding he leave Lake County within three days and resign his office. They had, however, taken his horse. A stiff knee prevented Dyer from simply walking out. The committee again warned the judge to leave, and this time he insisted on the return of his horse. They brought the animal, and the judge departed immediately for Fairplay in South Park. But after a few miles, he was stopped by two of the armed guards instructed not to let anyone pass in either direction. Finally, one of the guards let him by. Dyer was now extra cautious and stayed off the main road. For many miles he traveled cross-country through deep snow and finally reached Fairplay.

Dyer rode on to Denver and told his story to the newspapers. The press accused public officials, especially Governor John L. Routt, of taking no action to quell the disturbances in Lake County. Yielding to public opinion, Acting Governor John W. Heakins issued an official proclamation on February 5, calling upon the lawless people of Lake County to disperse. A private detective of considerable note, General David J. Cook, was sent to investigate. Much to everyone's surprise, Cook sent back an official report stating that order had been restored in the county. He was also assured by Lake County residents that no further trouble would occur. Cook seemed to justify the formation of the Committee of Safety by stating that it was originally organized as a posse to assist the sheriff in arresting the murderer of George Harrington. According to Cook, the posse evolved into a group of individuals set on investigating alleged cattle theft and the conduct of certain public officials. After the committee had served its purpose, it disbanded. Unfortunately, Cook failed to properly assess the state of affairs in Lake County, and his report turned out to be superficial.

The committee ordered a county commissioner and the county clerk to resign because they were friends of Gibbs. Suspects who refused to answer the committee's questions to its satisfaction were hung almost to death. According to the newspapers, around forty people had been run out of the county by the committee.

On April 1, Charles M. Harding[3] was found dead on the bank of the Arkansas River at Bales Station (near the present town of Salida). Harding had been a friend of Gibbs and had been warned by the committee to leave the county in thirty days. He swore he would rather die than be driven off.

Rev. Dyer appealed to Governor Routt to take steps to prevent further violence in Lake County. When the governor refused, Dyer appealed to the territorial representatives. He tried to get a bill introduced to place Lake County under the jurisdiction of some stronger county, but the measure was defeated.

During the spring of 1875, Judge Dyer returned to Granite in Lake County. Jesse Marion, who had escaped from the clutches of the committee after having been hung nearly to death, also returned with the judge to swear out warrants. The warrants were signed for the arrest of Dr. W. A. Dobbins and A. R. Strickland. During the proceedings, Sheriff Weldon and nearly thirty members of the Committee of Safety entered the courtroom fully armed, as a show of force. The effect was immediate. Marion was intimidated and became afraid to testify, forcing Judge Dyer to adjourn until the following morning. For the judge's own safety, he slept in the courtroom, which was located in a second-story room over a store.

At eight o'clock in the morning on July 3, the court reconvened and the accused members of the committee were dismissed due to lack of evidence. After the trial, Judge Dyer remained in the courtroom with a visitor. The man was called out of the room, and no sooner had he left than five men walked up the steps. Four shots were fired. One ball struck the judge's chair and another went through his arm above the wrist, then out the window. Cries of "spare my life" were heard in the street below. Evidently, the judge was held while a pistol was placed close to his head and fired; the hair around the bullet hole behind his ear was burned. The five assassins left the room. Another man rushed upstairs to the judge's side and heard him take his last few breaths.

Testimony was presented before a six-man coroner's jury. Witnesses recalled seeing the five men on the steps of the courthouse just prior to the shooting. Among the witnesses were Dr. Dobbins, Sheriff Weldon, and J. A. Woodward. Of these witnesses, only Woodward was willing to reveal the identity of the armed men. Woodward said he overheard threats made against the judge prior to the killing. Before he could testify, Woodward was shot to death.[4] Dead men don't talk.

Upon hearing that Judge Dyer had been killed, Governor Routt offered a two hundred dollar reward from territory funds to bring Dyer's murderers to justice. A Fairplay resident

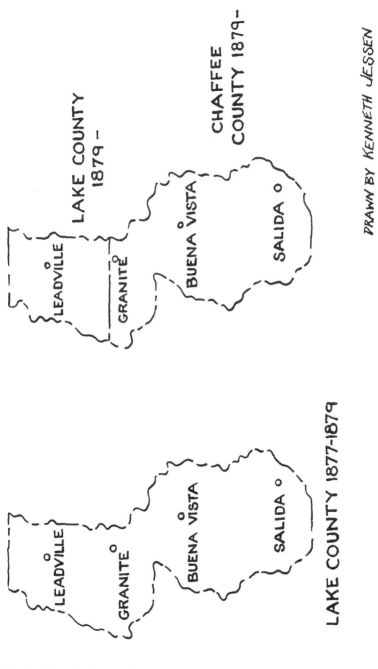

LAKE COUNTY
1879 –

LEADVILLE

GRANITE

BUENA VISTA

SALIDA

CHAFFEE
COUNTY 1879–

DRAWN BY KENNETH JESSEN

LEADVILLE

GRANITE

BUENA VISTA

SALIDA

LAKE COUNTY 1877-1879

officially requested the governor's help in restoring law and order to Lake County. The governor stalled by asking for more information, even after it was evident that Judge Dyer had died attempting to serve warrants on members of the Committee of Safety. In the *Daily Central City Register,* Sheriff Weldon was publicly accused of complicity in Judge Dyer's murder. This report put pressure on Governor Routt to do more than just post a reward. The governor wrote a letter calling for federal troops but failed to send it. He did send a lengthy confidential letter to General W. T. Sherman in St. Louis, outlining the events that took place. The general was asked to provide assistance in the form of a company of cavalry under the direction of a "discreet" officer. Because local law enforcement was involved in the mob rule, no local court of law could be effective in bringing things under control.

The problem was solved in 1879 when the major portion of Lake County that was involved in the struggle became part of Chaffee County. New officials were elected, a new judicial system was set up, and the disturbances stopped. The Lake County War ended with an estimated dozen residents dead.

Notes

1. In an account given by Henry Weber in 1934 and published in Ruby Williamson's *The Lake County War,* pp. 11–12, a bundle of hay was used as a shield instead of a horse.

2. Rev. John L. Dyer, in his book *The Snow-Shoe Itinerant,* states that one man was wounded by a shotgun that was accidentally discharged by one of the members of the mob.

3. The name is spelled "Hardin" in *The Snow-Shoe Itinerant.*

4. Woodard's death is mentioned in Rev. Dyer's account, but not by historian John Ophus in his article "The Lake County War, 1874-75."

References

Dyer, J. L. *Snow-Shoe Itinerant.* Cincinnati, Ohio: Cranston & Stoe, 1890, pp. 285–321. Reprint. Breckenridge, Colo.: Father Dyer United Methodist Church, 1976.

Ophus, John. "The Lake County War, 1874-75. *Colorado Magazine* 47, no. 2 (April 1970): 119-182.

Rasch, Philip J. "The Lake County (Colorado) War." *Real West* (February 1984): 10-13, 56.

Williamson, Ruby G. *The Lake County War.* Buena Vista, Colo.: Congregational United Church of Christ, 1976.

The character of early Pueblo is shown in this 1870 photograph of Santa Fe Avenue. It was through the streets of this town that Johnson and Clodfelter fled in their attempt to escape from detectives David Cook and Frank Smith. *Western History Department, Denver Public Library*

The Johnson and Clodfelter Manhunt

M ail swindles are not new. In fact, the Denver post office was aware, in August 1874, that a confidence game was being carried on by John W. Johnson and his associate, Ike Clodfelter. However, evidence was difficult to gather despite the complaints that rolled in. A plan was put together by law officers to trap Johnson.

The con involved circulars sent to likely individuals, which advertised good watches for only three dollars. When the unsuspecting parties sent in the money, all they received were bags of worthless stones or sawdust. Many people were too embarrassed to complain, and the extent of the swindle was never known.

Johnson's headquarters were at Island Station, about fifteen miles northeast of Denver along the South Platte River. Deputy Sheriff Wilcox was sent out to arrest him. (Wilcox was first made a U.S. marshal, since mail fraud is a federal offense.) Wilcox arrived at Island Station before the day's mail and waited for Johnson to come in. Soon Johnson and his partner, Ike Clodfelter, walked in to collect a registered letter sent by the post office to trap him. As soon as he received it, Wilcox stepped up and arrested him. Wilcox asked Johnson to turn over his weapon, and a pistol was promptly surrendered. The marshal now assumed that his man was disarmed. Johnson was permitted to go the door of the post office and leave some instructions about having his horse cared for.

This was a mistake. As soon as he reached the door, he ran, drawing a second concealed revolver from his boot. Wilcox chased him, drawing his own revolver, but he dropped it in the street. Still assuming his man was unarmed, Wilcox continued to chase Johnson.

Johnson ran hard and was followed by the marshal. As the marshal began to gain on him, Johnson cocked his pistol and

Deputy Sheriff Wilcox was shot by Ike Clodfelter while John Johnson held the lawman. This incident occurred at Island Station, northeast of Denver, when Wilcox was trying to arrest Johnson for mail fraud. *From Cook,* Hands Up!, *1897 ed.*

fired over his shoulder. The lead ball whizzed by Wilcox's head. The astonished marshal continued the chase, although his own firearm lay back in the dust in front of the post office. Johnson, on the other hand, did not know Wilcox was unarmed. Johnson continued to run and fire over his shoulder until five of his six chambers were empty.

Marshal Wilcox now assumed Johnson had discharged all of his rounds, since it was not wise to carry a revolver with all six chambers loaded. Accidental discharge of the weapon was possible if the gun was dropped. Johnson slowed to allow the marshal to come within a foot or two, then he fired again. Wilcox was shot in the groin, the ball passing through the fleshy part of his leg. He began to bleed badly. The two men struggled, and Johnson hit the marshal over the head with his empty revolver. The law officer called for the help of the postmaster as he pushed Johnson back toward the post office. Postmaster Fowler started out to help the wounded marshal, but Clodfelter drew his revolver and held Fowler at bay.

The struggle continued, and Johnson finally asked Clodfelter to shoot the marshal. Clodfelter refused but gave Johnson his loaded revolver and said, "Shoot the son of a bitch yourself." With a quick move, Wilcox injured Johnson's arm such that he couldn't fire. Clodfelter took his weapon back, and the marshal realized he was in a desperate struggle for his life. He fell to the ground and tried to throw Johnson off his feet to prevent being stomped in the head. Clodfelter stepped back about four feet and fired. Wilcox was seriously wounded in the back and continued to bleed from his first wound. The two desperadoes mounted their horses and fled.

General David J. Cook of the Rocky Mountain Detective Agency, along with the postmaster and the local sheriff, found Wilcox hanging onto his life by a slender thread. Wilcox was taken to Denver for treatment. News of the brutal shooting spread rapidly, and soon a reward of $250 was posted on a handbill. A manhunt was on.

Johnson and Clodfelter were seen about twenty-one miles south of Denver by a man who lived on Spring Creek. He recognized them from one of the handbills. The two men had asked him how to get to Pueblo without passing through Colorado Springs.

This photograph of General David J. Cook was made just two years prior to his death. He is best remembered as the head of the Rocky Mountain Detective Agency. He also served as Arapahoe County sheriff and Denver's city marshal. *Colorado Historical Society*

The reward for the capture of Johnson and Clodfelter climbed, with additional money offered by the territory, Arapahoe County, the postal service, and the Rocky Mountain Detective Agency for a total of seventeen hundred dollars.

General Cook and his partner, Frank Smith, left Denver on a Denver & Rio Grande train. As they traveled south on the narrow-gauge railroad, they inquired about the two hunted men at every station along the way. At Larkspur they found a man who said the fugitives had eaten supper the evening before at a home near the town. At Kelly Switch, the officers received another clue. They learned the two were headed over the Templeton Pass road, which split off from the main north-south route twelve miles south of Colorado Springs. At Colorado Springs, the detectives persuaded Mr. Rickerman, a local miller, to head over the road while the detectives continued south on the train to the point where the road rejoined the main route along Fountain Creek. They hoped to trap the two men somewhere along the road. The plan didn't work. Rickerman met the detectives, telling them that the two men had headed west toward Canon City. While Rickerman rode on, Cook and Smith walked the five miles to the town of Fountain.

Night came, and a severe March snowstorm hit hard. The snow was wet and heavy as it blew in from the north. At Fountain, the officers tried to purchase horses, but simply couldn't talk any of the ranchers into selling their animals. The prospects for continuing the chase looked gloomy. The officers were wet and cold, and the wagon road was now a sea of mud, making foot travel next to impossible.

A ray of hope broke on the scene when a posse of five men from Colorado Springs rode up in search of Johnson and Clodfelter. They were mounted on fine horses and were heavily armed with carbines and pistols. The group was headed by a deputy sheriff. Cook and Smith began to negotiate with the posse, suggesting a split of the reward money if two members would remain behind and give up their horses. The Colorado Springs officers held a brief meeting to discuss the proposal and flatly refused. The deputy sheriff concluded by saying, "You are out of luck, boys. Hope you will do better next time."

Under the circumstances, Cook and Smith had to try hard to maintain their composure. They ate dinner with the posse, and afterwards, the five men mounted their horses. The deputy

Frank Smith

Detective Frank Smith quite often went with General David Cook on his adventures. He was one of Cook's most trusted men in the Rocky Mountain Detective Agency. *Colorado Historical Society*

sheriff came over to Cook and his partner and asked, "Say, old fellow, which way do you think they went?"

It was now Cook's turn to have the upper hand, and he replied, "Give us two horses and I will tell you; without the horses I don't know a damn thing."

To this, the leader laughed, saying, "All right, we'll get 'em." Rickerman joined the posse, and they rode off in the direction of Canon City, much to the delight of the Denver detectives. They reasoned their men were headed south toward Pueblo and, based on their hunch, pressed on in the blinding snowstorm.

Late that night, for the sake of survival, Cook and Smith asked a rancher to give them a ride in his wagon. At a ranch, they learned that the men they were after had passed through the area that afternoon. The detectives walked over to the railroad track, where they noticed a section gang. They tried to persuade the men to take them to Pueblo in a handcar. Cook even attempted bribery by offering the men thirty dollars (equal to fifteen days pay on the railroad). However, the railroad men stuck to the rules, which forbade placing a handcar on the track at night.

Cook's response was, "If you don't put in on, we will. We must have it." The response from the section gang was the same as before: rules could not be broken. To this, Cook drew his revolver and said, "You can't, eh? Now, we've got to have the car. We're officers and must have it."

This was the first show of force on this case by the Denver detectives. The section men were astonished, and a compromise was reached. They agreed to take the detectives seven miles south, which was fourteen miles north of Pueblo. Aided by three of the workers, the detectives started out on the handcar. The officers and section gang alternately worked the lever to propel the car through the night and held brooms to the rails ahead of the wheels to prevent the car from derailing.

Eventually, Smith and Cook reached the ranch of John Irvine, where they were able to rent his wagon and team for twenty dollars. On to Pueblo the officers traveled, arriving at around three o'clock in the morning. Wet and exhausted, they managed to get a couple of local law officers who had seen the handbill to act as guards at the bridge over the Arkansas River between Pueblo and South Pueblo. Next, Cook and Smith rented a room and rested. With a hot fire going in the fireplace, they stretched out in their wet clothes, knowing that they might be called at any moment to continue the chase.

At around 6:00 A.M., the weary officers got up and began looking for horses. They finally found two animals and started north up the Fountain Creek road, thinking they were well ahead of Johnson and Clodfelter. Cook was armed with his Colt .44-caliber revolver and a Winchester lever-action rifle[2] he had borrowed in Pueblo. Smith had only his revolver.

The detectives had ridden only about two hundred yards from their hotel when they heard one of the officers guarding the bridge shout. Looking back, they could see the man waving at them, and in the distance, they could also see Johnson and Clodfelter riding south down Main Street toward the bridge. Cook and Smith wheeled their horses about and headed toward the bridge at a full gallop. They failed to cut off the fugitives, and now Johnson and Clodfelter realized they were being pursued. A chase through the streets of South Pueblo began, with Cook yelling, "If you don't halt, you are dead men." The fugitives pushed on, with their horses flying over the ground.

Cook had the presence of mind to leave word in Pueblo for Sheriff Ellis to follow as soon as he could. Cook then told his partner, "Let them have one just to scare them." The officers sent two shots into the air over the fleeing men, but it had no effect. The detectives swung around in a circle to gain high ground on a mesa. Cook stopped his horse, cocked his borrowed rifle, and drew a bead on one of the men, who was now only about sixty yards away. He pulled the trigger, but there was just a click. The gun was jammed. Smith, seeing that Cook's weapon wouldn't fire, poured six shots at the men. One of the shots grazed Johnson's leg, but the men continued to ride hard for open country.

The chase continued across the prairie, up small hills and down through gullies. Both the pursuers and the pursued threw away their coats, gloves, scarves, and even their holsters. Cook carried the rifle, and Smith, having the faster horse, rode ahead. Smith would stop, dismount, and grab the rifle as Cook rode up. Smith would then try to get off a good shot, but time and time again the rifle jammed. Cook finally gave his revolver to Smith and tried to fix the rifle while riding. He pulled out one cartridge and tried to insert another, but it stuck. Finally he forced it into the chamber just as his horse jumped over a

Denver detectives General David Cook and Frank Smith chased Clodfelter and Johnson across open country in a running gunfight near Pueblo. Clodfelter was eventually hit in the hand, and the pair surrendered to the lawmen. *From Cook,* Hands Up!, *1897 ed.*

sagebrush plant. The horse landed with one hind foot in a prairie dog hole, and Cook was thrown forward. Injured in the groin, Cook rode on as he tried to fix the rifle. The officers came within range and got off two shots, but with no effect.

At that point, Johnson and Clodfelter turned away toward Canon City and rode across the open ground. The horses plunged through snow banks. The sun was blinding as the chase continued. Both parties began to weaken. The fugitives' horses were so tired they could not be whipped out of a trot. The officers were now able to come within sixty yards, and Cook shouted, "See here boys, this thing has gone about far enough. Your horses are broken down. We are well heeled, and if you don't stop, we'll kill you. You may count on it." The pair paid no attention, and the detectives fired several more rounds at them.

The third shot went through Clodfelter's hand near the knuckle of the third finger, and the slug penetrated down to his elbow. It also blew his Colt Navy percussion revolver in half, leaving a deep mark where the brass frame met the barrel. At the time, he was holding the pistol around the cylinder and pounding his exhausted horse with it. When Clodfelter was hit, his horse reeled, and the desperado fell to the ground. He called to Johnson, "We must surrender. It's no use. I'm shot." Johnson dismounted and threw his hands up, tossing his revolver away.

The two detectives dismounted and walked up to the men cautiously. Johnson was standing with his hands raised while Clodfelter lay on the ground by his horse. The horse was blowing so hard it could be heard clearly for some distance.

There was a moment of silence. Cook addressed Johnson, "You surrender, do you?"

"We do," was his reply.

"Have you got another pistol?"

"I have just thrown it away," was Johnson's elusive answer.

"But have you another one? You don't want any Wilcox business on us. I will have you searched," Cook continued in a determined voice. "And if another weapon is found on you, I will kill you where you stand. Do you understand?"

Very slowly, Johnson reached into a concealed pocket and produced a second revolver with his thumb and forefinger. He dropped it to the ground. Clodfelter said he was armed but was

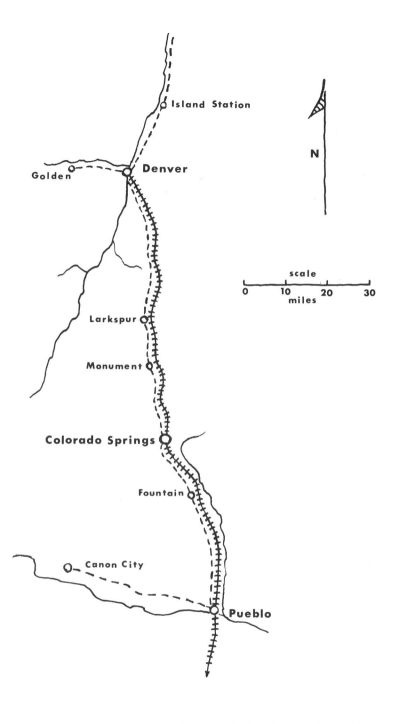

Island Station

Golden Denver

N

scale
0   10   20   30
miles

Larkspur

Monument

Colorado Springs

Fountain

Canon City

Pueblo

so badly wounded he couldn't remove his weapon. After being disarmed, Clodfelter fainted from loss of blood.

As the men were about to start toward Pueblo, they spotted a string of horsemen coming their way. It was Sheriff Ellis and his posse. All of the men returned together to Pueblo, and almost the entire town came out to greet them. Johnson bragged he would never have been captured had his partner not been wounded. Clodfelter sang another tune, saying again and again that he was sorry for what he had done.

The detectives left on a northbound train and arrived in Colorado Springs where they also received a royal reception. This was followed by another in Denver. A heavily armed posse was required to guarantee the safe passage of the prisoners to the Arapahoe County jail.

Johnson and Clodfelter were tried for murder, but since Wilcox's wounds did not prove fatal, they were sent to the state penitentiary on a lesser charge for three and a half years.

Notes

1. The account given in the Pueblo *Colorado Chieftain* stated that Johnson gave his revolver to his partner and that he broke away from Wilcox and ran out the door.

2. Although this is a rather minor point, the *Colorado Chieftain* said that David J. Cook used a Henry lever-action rifle rather than a Winchester.

References

[Dawson, Thomas Fulton?] *Hands Up! or Twenty Years of Detective Life in the Mountains and on the Plains.* Denver: W. F. Robinson Printing Co., 1882. Reprint. Norman, Okla: University of Oklahoma Press, 1958, pp. 289-307.

"The Pursuit of Johnson and Gladfelty [sic]." Pueblo *Colorado Chieftain*, March 4, 1875, p. 1, cols. 2-4.

Clay Allison was one of the West's best-known gunfighters. He is pictured here at the age of twenty-six. *Western History Collection, University of Oklahoma Library*

Clay Allison's
Last Gunfight

O n December 21, 1876, Clay Allison and his brother, John, had traveled from their home in Cimarron, New Mexico, to Las Animas, Colorado. They were on a drinking spree at the Olympic Dance Hall. Bent County Sheriff John Spiers had been alerted that the Allisons were in town. They had visited Las Animas a little over a year before, threatening to take over the town and waving their pistols. The sheriff elected to leave the brothers alone unless there was a repeat of their wild actions.

But the Allisons didn't behave. They intentionally trampled on the toes of some of the women in the dance hall, trying to provoke a fight. Their actions prompted Deputy Charles Faber to visit the Olympic and ask the Allisons to check their guns. They flatly refused and continued to make trouble.

Faber left the Olympic but soon returned with a borrowed double-barreled shotgun. He was determined to disarm the Allison brothers. He took two deputies with him just in case there was trouble. When Faber entered the hall, Clay was standing at the bar with his back to the entrance, while John was at the end of the hall dancing.

With little warning, Faber fired at John just as someone shouted, "Look out!" John turned and was struck in the chest and shoulder by the shotgun blast. Seeing his brother collapse to the floor, Clay returned the fire. The first bullet may very well have killed Faber,[1] but Clay continued to pump round after round into the deputy's body. As Faber fell, the second barrel of his shotgun discharged, wounding John Allison a second time.

The other deputies fled out the door, with Clay in hot pursuit. He fired at them as they ran down the street. Clay returned to his badly wounded brother, then dragged Faber's lifeless body over to him and said, "John, here's the man that shot you, look at the Goddamn son of a bitch. I killed him!" As his brother was being moved out of the dance hall to his hotel

Clay Allison's last gunfight took place in Las Animas, Colorado, on December 21, 1876. This photo of Las Animas was taken two years earlier. *Colorado Historical Society*

room, Clay struck the corpse on the head and said again, "John, here's the damned son of a bitch that shot you, and I killed him."

John and Clay had taken a room in the Vandiver House. Sheriff Spiers was notified of his deputy's death and went to the Vandiver to arrest the brothers. Clay was preoccupied with his brother's chance of surviving and surrendered without a struggle. John was moved to the second story of the jail, which also served as an infirmary, while Clay was locked up on the ground floor. At first, John's wounds in the breast and leg were considered critical, and many doubted he would survive. Some of the buckshot had passed almost through his body and had to be removed through his back. Slowly, however, John began to recover.

A coroner's jury was summoned, and an inquest was held the following day. The jury concluded that Faber met his death while performing his official duty. They also said that the deputy's death was premeditated by the Allisons. On January 8, Clay was taken before a judge in West Las Animas. The original charge of murder was changed to manslaughter.

On January 9, the Pueblo *Colorado Daily Chieftain* expressed its opinion on the matter:

> Mr. Allison thinks his brother, who was shot by Faber with a double-barreled shotgun, will not recover. Whether the courts will sustain officers in slipping up behind men and shooting them without a word of warning remains to be seen.[2]

John Allison was released on February 3 for lack of evidence. He was still recovering from his wounds. A grand jury determined Clay had acted in self-defense, and he was also released.[3]

Clay Allison was one of the West's best-known gunfighters. He was born in Tennessee and, after the Civil War, took up land in Texas. He then moved to New Mexico. Clay was involved in a number of gunfights prior to the incident with Deputy Faber. For example, he participated in the mob killing of Charles Kennedy in Elizabethtown, New Mexico; he killed John Colber and Francisco Griego in Cimarron, New Mexico; and, with some of his friends, he also killed three soldiers.

Ironically, Clay Allison died in a freak accident. He was in Pecos, Texas, getting supplies for his ranch on July 1, 1887. As he headed back home a sack of feed on the wagon began to slide off. Allison lost his balance trying to keep the sack on the wagon and fell under its wheels. The heavily loaded wagon passed over his neck and head.

His grave in Pecos Park, next to the West of the Pecos Museum, has two markers, one of wood and the other of granite. They read respectively, "Clay Allison, Gentleman Gunfighter, 1840-1887, R. I. P." and "Robert Clay Allison, 1840-1887, He Never Killed a Man that did not Need Killing."

Notes

1. According to other accounts, Clay fired four shots, but only the first one hit Faber. See Dale T. Schenberger's *The Gunfighters*, p. 13.

2. The Las Animas *Leader*, January 12, 1877, took exception to this statement in an article titled, "Blackening the Memory of the Dead."

3. In *The Gunfighters*, p. 13, Schoenberger says Clay was released "on the ground no bill had been found against him" and no witnesses could be produced to testify against him.

References

"Blackening the Memory of the Dead." Las Animas *Leader*, January 12, 1877, p. 2, col. 1.

Breiham, Carl W. *Great Gunfighters of the West*. San Antonio, Tex.: The Naylor Co., 1962, pp. 154-167.

"Clay Allison Admitted to Bail." Pueblo *Colorado Chieftain*, January 9, 1877.

"Constable Faber Killed—The Allison Brothers Made a Raid on West Animas." Las Animas *Leader*, December 22, 1876, p. 3, col. 2.

Parsons, Chuck. *Clay Allison, Portrait of a Shootist*. Seagraves, Tex.: Pioneer Book Publishers, 1983, pp. 30-31.

———. *Shadows Along the Pecos*. Pecos, Tex.: West of the Pecos Museum, 1977, p. 21.

Pueblo *Colorado Chieftain,* December 27, 1876, p. 4, col. 2; December 31, 1876, p. 4, col. 3.

Schoenberger, Dale T. *The Gunfighters.* Caldwell, Idaho: Caxton Printers, Ltd., 1971, pp. 12–13.

Samuel Woodruff and Joseph Seminole killed R. B. Hayward and stole his wagon. This began a massive manhunt. After Woodruff and Seminole were captured and placed in a Golden jail, a lynch mob served out the final punishment. *From Cook*, Hands Up!, *1897 ed.*

Double Lynching in Golden

In August 1879, police officers in Denver were told in a dispatch from the sheriff of Grand County to keep a sharp eye out for a man who was wanted for the robbery of Frank Byers, a prominent Middle Park rancher. They were told the man might be part Indian. The robbery took place on the eighth, and on the twelfth, a second incident occurred near Georgetown. The same man had given his name as Joseph F. Seminole and had called upon a local doctor. He told the doctor that a lady in Hot Sulphur Springs was quite ill and needed immediate medical attention. The doctor was instructed by Joseph Seminole to stop six miles out of town on the road to Empire and pick up a mule left with a local rancher. Seminole appeared thoughtful and sincere. The doctor was told that a durable mule was much more suitable for the trip than his fine horse. At the summit of Berthoud Pass, he was to present a note to the proprietor of the Summit House. The note would allow the doctor to secure a rig to continue his journey.

When the doctor reached the ranch, he found the mule, and he did as he had been instructed, leaving his horse behind. He continued on to the Summit House atop Berthoud Pass and presented the note to the proprietor. To his surprise, the proprietor had never heard of Seminole. He did, however, loan the doctor a horse and buggy for his mission of mercy. When the doctor reached the home of the woman, however, she was as well as could be. The doctor was astonished. Back he traveled over Berthoud Pass until he finally reached the ranch where he had left his fine horse. But Seminole had used this elaborate scheme to steal the doctor's horse and had fled the area.

On September 7, Seminole surfaced in Leadville with a partner, Samuel Woodruff, who traveled under the alias of Tom Johnson. Woodruff was a stonecutter by trade and had served three years for killing a man. He had become intimate with the man's wife.

The two men hired horses for what they claimed would be a little ride. While riding around Leadville, they noticed a Mr. Aldrich drawing two hundred dollars from a local bank. They learned that Aldrich planned to travel to Georgetown on the other side of the Continental Divide. It was a perfect opportunity for Seminole and Woodruff, and they followed Aldrich through the mountains waiting for the right moment. After a full day's ride and just six miles from Georgetown, they drew their revolvers and commanded Aldrich to halt. Aldrich was prepared for highwaymen and quickly drew his own weapon. He immediately began firing. Seminole and Woodruff had to flee for their lives.

When Aldrich arrived in Georgetown, he notified the sheriff of Clear Creek County. The sheriff set out after the men and began to gain on them. To escape, the desperadoes dismounted and fled into the dense timber.

On September 10, Seminole and Woodruff walked up to the home of a man named Anderson. They hired him to take them to Denver, making up a story that they didn't have any money and that an uncle in Denver would pay for the ride. Anderson noticed during the course of the trip that the men did have some money and insisted that they pay the toll charges. They refused, and Anderson said he would take them no farther. A pair of cocked revolvers persuaded him to change his mind. About a mile down the road, a couple of wagons approached. Seminole and Woodruff jumped from Anderson's wagon and ran into the timber. They evidently feared that Anderson would call for help. Anderson turned his wagon, joined the other wagons for safety, and returned home.

Later in the day, the two outlaws came to the home of R. B. Hayward. Hayward was a peaceful fellow with a loving wife and two daughters. They hired Hayward to take them to a cattle camp that they claimed was near Green Mountain. The trip involved traveling down Mt. Vernon Canyon on the toll road to Denver. The men rode in the back of the wagon with Hayward on the driver's seat. Woodruff suddenly grabbed Hayward around the throat and choked him to death. They then pushed the body off the wagon and stuffed it under a small bridge.

Mrs. Hayward offered $200 for the capture of her husband's killer. This reward was followed by another of $500 from Jefferson County. To this, Governor Pitkin added $1,000 from state funds, bringing the price on the head of the murderer to $1,700 (worth more than $17,000 in today's dollars).

In Denver, the wagon was sold for $190. The men then hired a buggy with two bay mares at Brown & Marr's "bus barn" on Arapahoe Street. They paid $4 in advance and told the proprietor that they just wanted to take a little spin around town.

The following morning the two men abandoned the buggy near Loveland and rode off bareback on the mares. Near LaPorte they talked a local rancher out of a couple of buffalo robes, which they claimed would be used to allow them to camp in the area. They told the rancher they had been hired to round up stray cattle and would return the robes. The rancher never saw his robes again.

The two men were spotted next by a rancher between Laramie and Cheyenne on September 22. They were easily recognized because of the buffalo robes and the bay mares. The rancher was asked where he lived. This made him suspicious, and he played dumb. The rancher later reported the men to a local law officer.

A day or so later, Seminole and Woodruff were seen near Sidney, Nebraska. Detective W. N. Ayers from Denver was sent after them, but at the time, law officers did not know for sure if Seminole and Woodruff were connected to Hayward's death.

Seminole was a half-breed Sioux, and Detective Ayers reasoned that he was headed home to the Pine Ridge Indian Agency in South Dakota. It was a journey of roughly five hundred miles. Ayers traveled to the agency by way of Cheyenne; Fort Robinson, Nebraska (near Crawford); and Camp Sheridan. When he reached the reservation, he used letters of identification to secure the help of the Indian police. Ayers found out that Seminole lived there under the name J. S. Leuischammesse, and he was soon led to the wigwam of the culprit.

Seminole was found relaxing in Indian fashion with his squaw and children. He looked quite at peace puffing on a traditional long-stemmed pipe. When Ayers introduced himself as an officer from Colorado, Seminole showed no sign of alarm. After all, anything could happen during the course of the long

Denver detective W. N. Ayers rode all the way to the Pine Ridge Indian Agency in South Dakota to capture Seminole. Indian police had to aid in the capture when Seminole began to struggle. *From Cook,* Hands Up!, *1897 ed.*

journey back to Denver. It was one thing to arrest a man and quite another to bring him to justice.

When Seminole was taken outside his wigwam, Ayers attempted to handcuff him. Seminole now showed signs of resisting arrest. He was bigger and stronger than the law officer, and it took the Indian police to bring the half-breed down.

An armed escort of Sioux Indians accompanied Ayers and his prisoner back toward the Wyoming border. At Camp Robinson, south of the agency, his escort left. The pair traveled to Pine Bluffs, Wyoming, east of Cheyenne. Here Ayers persuaded a Union Pacific train crew to allow him and his prisoner to ride in the caboose of a freight train back to Denver.

At three o'clock in the morning the following day, the law officer discovered that his prisoner had jumped from the moving freight as it sped through the darkness. Ayers had not dreamt that a handcuffed man would even attempt such a feat. Everything seemed lost; nevertheless, Ayers telegraphed law officers in Cheyenne. A group of fifteen cowboys was soon looking for Seminole, under the direction of a local sheriff. Nine hours from the time he jumped from the train, Seminole was recaptured.

As soon as the half-breed was locked up in the county jail in Denver, Hayward's widow was asked to walk down a row of prisoners that included Seminole and look at each one. When she came to Seminole, she exclaimed, "My God! That's the man. Take him away from me." Seminole was also identified by a man from the Brown & Marr stables. With this type of evidence against him, the half-breed made a full confession.

His partner, Woodruff, alias Tom Johnson, was still at large. Detective W. N. Ayers was sent out after this man. Detective C. A. Hawley accompanied Ayers, since it was believed that Woodruff's capture would be far more difficult than Seminole's had been. The two detectives began tracking a man answering Woodruff's description in western Nebraska, but it took another week of tracking to catch him. Returning to Denver in mid-November, the detectives discovered that their prisoner was indeed wanted, but that he was not Woodruff.

Hawley was sent out alone to look up Samuel Woodruff's relatives in eastern Nebraska. In the meantime, the newspapers reported that Tom Johnson had been captured and taken to Denver to stand trial. Hawley hoped that Woodruff would read

Samuel Woodruff was captured in Big Grove, Iowa, by Denver detective C. A. Hawley with the help of a local law officer. Woodruff was living with his brother James. *From Cook,* Hands Up!, *1897 ed.*

the newspaper article about his capture and become careless. Using an assumed name, Hawley found that a James W. Woodruff lived in Big Grove, Iowa, about thirty miles from Council Bluffs. Hawley also learned that Samuel, James Woodruff's brother, was living with James and had a bank account of nine thousand dollars.

After locating the Woodruff home in Big Grove, Hawley returned to Council Bluffs. On November 25, he swore out a warrant before a local justice of the peace. With a constable, Hawley set out in a buggy for the Woodruff home. The next morning, after concealing their rig, the two men walked into Big Grove, looking more like tramps than officers.

The brothers soon became aware of the two strangers in their small town. The Woodruffs walked down the main street together with James carrying an ax and Samuel a revolver. Using a borrowed double-barreled shotgun, Hawley waited in a local store for the men to approach. When they were within range, he pulled back the hammers on the shotgun and stepped out into the street. He brought the weapon up to his shoulder and said, "Sam Woodruff, throw up your hands; I want you."

Sam began to bring his revolver up to fire when Hawley said, "Pull that pistol one inch and I'll blow daylight through you." Sam dropped his weapon and put up his hands. He was placed in irons, and in a few minutes, the officers were on their way back to Council Bluffs with their prisoner. Hawley continued his journey with Sam Woodruff, and when they arrived in Cheyenne a number of people were able to identify the outlaw. The two men traveled on to Denver, and Samuel was placed in jail with his partner, Seminole.

On December 3, 1879, in a dramatic scene, Mrs. Hayward and her two daughters were brought into the parlor of the jail. They sat on a sofa facing the door to the cells. Woodruff was brought into the room and was promptly identified as one of the men who went off with Mr. Hayward. Next, Joseph Seminole was brought into the room and was identified for the second time.

Public indignation over the murder of an innocent man began to grow. The sweet little Hayward girls had been left without their father. It became common knowledge that Mr. Hayward was a fine, gentle man.

The prisoners were moved from the jail in Denver to the county jail in Golden. Christmas came and went, and the murderer had still not been brought to justice.

On Saturday night, December 27, a party of about thirty-five horsemen, accompanied by an equal number on foot, came down Golden's main street. A wagon, pulled by a double team and loaded with men, followed the horsemen. The procession could be seen clearly in the full moon. Not a word was spoken, and the only noises were the low rumble of the horses' hooves and the squeak of wagon springs. All of the men knew their job. They wore masks or handkerchiefs or had blackened their faces with burnt cork.

The mounted men blocked all the approaches to the jail. One man climbed a telegraph pole and cut the wires leading to the jail. There was no noise or confusion. Sledgehammers, cold chisels, crowbars, and other tools were taken from the wagon to the outer door of the jail.

The jailer, Edgar Cox, was asleep on a bench in the sheriff's office. He heard a noise outside and looked at the windows. In each one was framed the face of two or three men. The gleaming barrels of many guns pointed right at him. The heavy thump of twenty-five pairs of boots could be heard entering the jail, and he was told not to move.

The undersheriff, Joseph T. Boyd, was asleep in his quarters in the rear of the jail. The sound of hammers striking the lock to the cell door woke him up. Quickly he pulled on his clothes and rushed out into the front room, only to find it filled to capacity with masked, armed men. He knew immediately what was about to happen and made his way through the crowd to the stairs leading to the story above. He began to address the crowd, reminding them they they were about to take the law into their own hands. His appeal continued, saying that justice would be served.

His eloquence fell on deaf ears. As four or five revolvers pointed at his head, he was ordered to hold up his hands. He was then removed from the room. The jail keys were not requested; the men preferred to break the locks on the cell doors.

The assault on the jail door continued, as Woodruff and Seminole trembled with fear. Seminole cried out like a wild animal. Cold chisels cut into the padlocks on Woodruff's cell, and sledgehammers finished the job. Woodruff struggled against the men and was subdued by a few blows from the butt of a revolver. He was carried from his cell with blood running down his forehead and laid on his stomach. His wrists were bound behind his back as he cried out, "Gentlemen, you are mistaken. I am innocent of this crime."

When the knots were secured, Undersheriff Boyd came forward and asked what he could do for the prisoner. Woodruff requested that a letter be drafted to his wife and a second letter be written to his brother James. He added that he wanted his brother to avenge his death.

The next jail door to yield was Seminole's. A number of men entered the cell all at once. They found the condemned man lying on his face, moaning. He was carried out and bound like his partner. The two men were then taken out of the jail and partially pushed or carried three or four hundred yards over to the trestle of the Golden & South Platte Railroad, in full view of the courthouse.

At first, they were taken under the bridge and preparations were made to hang them. Woodruff begged them not to hang him by pulling him off the ground, but asked to be allowed to jump from the trestle. His request was granted. The noose was first placed around his neck, and he was led up the embankment to the top of the bridge. The other end of the rope was secured to a tie.

One of the masked men asked, "Sam Woodruff, do you wish to say anything?"

His reply was, "Gentlemen, you are hanging an innocent man, but I trust God will forgive you as I do. May I say my prayers?" Dressed in a dark, checkered shirt, duck overalls, and cotton socks, he knelt as best he could on the ties and prayed for perhaps a minute. When he was finished, he said, "I have one last request. Permit me to jump off the bridge; don't push me to my death." But as Woodruff stepped to the edge of the ties, two or three men gave him a slight push. His body fell the full length of the rope and stopped with a thud. It was all over for Woodruff.

Seminole was then brought to the top of the bridge. Several men placed a rope around his neck, and he was asked if he had anything to say. He replied, "Gentlemen, I have but little to say. . . . In relation to this murder, gentlemen, we two are the

The end came for Woodruff and Seminole in Golden on December 27, 1879, on a railroad trestle at the hands of a lynch mob. Woodruff pleaded for his life but was hung first. Before Seminole died, he admitted that they had killed Hayward. *From Cook,* Hands Up!, *1897 ed.*

guilty ones. We committed the crime. I have no excuse to offer, nothing to say." Contrary to this statement, he then began a long, emotional, and elaborate prayer. The members of the lynch mob, moved by his prayer, took off their hats and bowed their heads. Seminole concluded his prayer by saying, "Take me to Thee, sinful though I am."

Below, the body of his companion twitched. The rope about Seminole's neck drooped down towards the ties as he stood with one foot on the rail and the other on a tie. The details of this scene were made especially vivid by the moonlight on the cold December night. Seminole was dressed in a checkered vest and a dark sack coat over his undershirt. He wore dark pantaloons, brown socks, and Indian moccasins. Finally, after Seminole had exhausted all that he was going to say, he rose to his feet, trembling like an aspen leaf, and stood at the edge of the trestle. The fatal push was given, and he died instantly of a broken neck.

As soon as the bodies of the two men hung beneath the bridge in the stillness of the night, the crowd began to show signs of uneasiness, and many wanted to move away. The leader ordered them to stay until it was certain that the two murderers were dead. Finally, when there was no doubt that Woodruff and Seminole had taken their last breaths, the crowd moved away.

The mob rode to the south on Ford Street, and as they passed the home of widow Hayward near the corner of Tenth Street, the whole band came to a halt. Each man fired his revolver into the air and shouted, "Hayward is avenged!" The mob broke up, and each man returned to his home.

Shortly thereafter, Dr. Joseph Anderson, the coroner, arrived on the scene of the hanging. One of the members of the lynch mob had lingered behind and asked, "What are you doing?"

The doctor's reply was, "Examining into your devilish work."

"Are they dead?" asked the man.

"Yes; deader than hell," was the doctor's reply.

"All right, Hayward is avenged. Good night." The lone horseman rode off into the night.

Both men were buried in the Golden cemetery. The Denver *Tribune,* December 30, 1879, commented:

In wandering through the town of Golden, yesterday, and conversing with business men of all grades of social and intellectual standing, the reporter failed to find a solitary person who condemned this recent lynching. One every side the popular verdict seemed to be that the hanging was not only well merited, but a positive gain to the county, saving it at least five or six thousand dollars.

References

[Dawson, Thomas Fulton?] *Hands Up! or Twenty Years of Detective Life in the Mountains and on the Plains.* Denver: W. F. Robinson Printing Co., 1882. Reprint. Norman, Okla: University of Oklahoma Press, 1958, pp. 73–103.

"Illegally Hanged." Golden *Colorado Transcript,* December 31, 1879.

"The Vigilante's Work." Golden *Colorado Transcript,* December 31, 1879.

Leadville lawman Martin Duggan was the town's third marshal in just two months, but he managed to restore law and order. For his efforts he received $125 a month. *Western History Department, Denver Public Library*

Leadville Lawman Martin Duggan

The first marshal in Leadville was T. H. Harrison. He held the job only a few days, however, because threats from the lawless element convinced him he would live longer in some other location. On April 2, 1878, George O'Connor was elected by the city council to replace the prudent T. H. Harrison.

On April 25, Marshal O'Connor stopped at Billy Nye's saloon in the course of making his rounds. He was enjoying a mug of beer, courtesy of the management, when one of his junior officers, James M. Bloodsworth, approached him at the bar.

"I hear that you called me a coward and a guy," Bloodsworth said.

O'Connor promptly set the record straight by denying having said such a thing about one of his own men. Nevertheless, in an instant the junior officer drew his revolver and fired point blank at O'Connor. The first shot hit the marshal in the stomach, and the second hit him just below the heart. The impact threw O'Connor back against the bar. As O'Connor slumped to the barroom floor, Bloodsworth pumped three more rounds into his victim, then fled. Bloodsworth had his horse waiting and left Leadville, never to be seen again.

Mayor H.A.W. Tabor offered six hundred dollars for the arrest "and return of the body of James Bloodsworth." Marshal O'Connor lived a few hours, but even before he was dead, Mayor Tabor called a special meeting of the Leadville city council to replace the marshal. Martin Duggan, an Irishman, was appointed the new city marshal. Born in County Limerick, Duggan spent his boyhood on the streets of New York City. At sixteen, he headed west. In 1876, after trying his hand at ranching along the Platte River, Duggan went to Georgetown to try prospecting. His size and physical strength got him a job as a bouncer in the Occidental Dance Hall.

One night, a guest began shooting the candles out. Duggan put a stop to it by grabbing him by the scruff of the neck. Just as Duggan was about to pitch the man out, the guest shouted, "You can lick me with your fists, but you can't do it in a fair fight with guns. Gimme my shooter and I'll give you all the fun you want, you bully."

"I'm no bully," replied Duggan, "and if you must have a fight, I'll accommodate you. Come outside, and we'll settle it."

On the snow-covered road, the two men faced each other at twenty paces. A referee, standing in the doorway of the Occidental, raised his own revolver and fired a shot into the air. The two adversaries advanced toward each other, firing as they walked. Duggan's third shot put a hole in the man's breast. The man fell face first into the snow. This and several other incidents gave Duggan the reputation of a fearless man.

Marshal Duggan had his work cut out for him in Leadville. He was the town's third marshal in just two months. Soon Duggan received written notice to leave town within twenty-four hours or follow George O'Connor. The new marshal didn't let the threat interfere with his work, but he took every precaution and was on guard at all times. Law and order was a new concept in Leadville, and many a crusty miner did not want to have a stranger tell him how to act. Leadville also had a large lawless crowd.

Martin Duggan was of medium height but had a compact, massive build. He was very strong. He had a square face, a broad forehead, and fine features. His light hair and fair complexion complemented his blue eyes. As a lawman, Duggan was not overly concerned with "due process." He fought for law and order using the same methods as the lawless. He wasted no time in establishing his version of the law, and for his efforts, he received $125 a month.[1]

Duggan felt that everyone in Leadville should abide by the law, regardless of social standing. August Rische was Mayor Tabor's partner in the fabulous Little Pittsburgh mine. One evening, Rische became drunk and disorderly, and Mart Duggan hauled him in as he would any other Leadville citizen.[2]

The mayor was astonished when he learned about his partner's jail sentence. The following morning Tabor stopped by and asked Duggan, "I hear you got my business associate in your lock up?"

"That's right, Mr. Mayor," replied Duggan.

"What's the fine on him?" Tabor asked.

"No fine," was Duggan's terse reply.

Tabor still did not take Duggan seriously and told the marshal, "That's what I like, an understanding marshal. Give him a scare, a night in jail."

"He's in for ten days," was Duggan's next dry remark.

"Now look here, Duggan, I'm the mayor of this town," said the now irritated Tabor.

"And I'm the law here, Mr. Tabor. Rische owes the city of Leadville ten days." Duggan was unflinching. "You can pick him up when he's paid."

At that, Tabor threatened to relieve Duggan of his duties, to which the marshal replied, "Ten days. Now, Mr. Mayor, you best go do your mayorin' or I'll put you in too . . . disturbin' the peace and agitatin' the marshal." Tabor knew he had hired a good man, one with high principles.

Not long after the incident with Rische, a negro named John Elkins spent Sunday playing poker with some other men, including Charlie Hines, in the Pioneer Saloon on East Chestnut. The game broke up at midnight, and the players adjourned to the bar. An argument broke out between Elkins and Hines. Fists began to fly, but some friends broke up the fight. Later that morning, the pair met again, and their fight was resumed. Despite the fact that others tried to separate them, Elkins managed to bury his knife in Hines's mid-section, and in the confusion, Elkins escaped.

Hines was taken to the saloon's back room. He was near death as an angry mob formed to seek out and lynch John Elkins. The situation prompted one of the officers to race to Mart Duggan's home. He woke the marshal and explained what had happened. Other Leadville officers located Elkins at his girlfriend's home and took him to jail. Duggan dressed immediately and sped down a side street to get ahead of the mob.

When the crowd rounded the corner by the jail, which was a little over four blocks from the Pioneer Saloon, Marshal Duggan stood his ground under a street lamp, with a cocked revolver in each hand. He told the mob he would kill the first man who stepped by the lamp post. Out of the two hundred-some angry men in the crowd, a few shouted, "On to the jail."

Duggan made it perfectly clear that someone would be killed if they attempted to interfere with the law. By seeking out the leaders, Duggan was able to control the mob.

After a while, Hines recovered from his knife wound and a year later wound up working on the Leadville police force. As for Elkins, he was quietly released from jail and fled the area.

Despite Duggan's effectiveness at keeping others under control, he was not always successful at keeping himself under control. One February night in 1879, Duggan was with two companions at the Tontine. Duggan paid for his drink with a silver coin known as a "trade dollar." It was common practice to discount the trade dollar 25 percent. Bartender L. H. Beasy subtracted the percentage and returned the change to Duggan. The drunken marshal was outraged and became violent. He drew his revolver and threatened to kill Beasy. He went behind the bar and knocked the bartender to the floor, calling him vile names in the process. Duggan denounced the owners of the Tontine as thieves and robbers. Beasy later filed a formal complaint against the marshal, which resulted in Duggan's suspension. After a while, Beasy thought better of what he had done, dropped the charges, and left Leadville for good.

The Leadville *Chronicle* said of Martin Duggan, "Sober, there was no more courteous, obliging person. But under the influence of liquor, he was the incarnation of deviltry, and had as little regard for human life as a wild beast."

Marshal Mart Duggan's appointment ran out in April 1879, and he decided not to accept a second term. He and his wife traveled to Flint, Michigan, to visit her relatives. In the meantime, the rough element in Leadville began again to make itself known, as the new marshal was unable to keep things under control. After a particularly bad sequence of violent events, including a double lynching by citizens who realized that the Leadville police force was ineffective, a wire was sent to Duggan. He was asked to reconsider his decision to resign. In December, Mart Duggan was once again the Leadville city marshal. In April 1880, his second term expired, and again he refused to serve another term. He went into the livery business and indulged in horse racing.

On Monday, November 22, he was asked to deliver a sleigh to Winnie Purdy. She was one of Leadville's ladies of pleasure and lived in the red-light district. Duggan set out across the fresh snow in a sharp-looking sleigh pulled by a pair of equally good-looking black horses. As he neared the corner of Pine and Fifth he almost knocked down Louis Lamb. The two men exchanged a few heated words, and Duggan drove off. This should have ended the matter, but his hot Irish temper got the best of him, and Duggan turned the sleigh. Once he reached Lamb he demanded an apology. Lamb elected to let his revolver do his talking. This was a mistake because Duggan dropped to the ground behind one of his horses and shot Lamb through the mouth. Lamb died instantly and fell to the ground with his pistol still cocked. Duggan voluntarily surrendered to the police captain and later was found innocent by virtue of self-defense. Ironically, Duggan had never killed a man during his term as marshal.

Louis Lamb had been a local miner and a family man. His wife vowed eternal hatred for the ex-marshal, and she promised to wear her "widow's weeds" until Duggan was dead. She then vowed to dance on his grave and deliver her "widow's weeds" to Duggan's wife.

After Duggan killed Lamb, his business went downhill and finally failed in 1882. He left Leadville, only to return in 1887 to work as a policeman. In April of the following year, Duggan was at the Texas House, a popular Leadville gambling establishment, when he got into an argument with owner Bailey Youngson. Duggan was drunk and upset with one of the dealers for some unknown reason. He threatened to run the fellow out of town. When Youngson attempted to defend his dealer, Duggan asked him to get his gun and meet him out in the street.

Duggan's friends convinced him to leave and go home. At around half past three in the morning, a shot rang out, and several men began shouting for the police. They found Martin Duggan lying in a pool of his own blood on the boardwalk in front of the Texas House. A bullet had entered his head behind the right ear, and it was amazing that he was still alive. The powder burns indicated that he had been shot at close range.

When daylight came, Duggan regained consciousness. His mind seemed clear, and he asked for a drink of water. He turned toward a window and remarked, "It is light."

An officer was by his bed and asked in a whisper, "Who did it, Mart? Who shot you?"

Leadville's Texas House is the building with the awning in the center of this photograph. It was here that Martin Duggan was gunned down and Louis Lamb's widow danced for joy. *Colorado Historical Society*

In a strong, clear voice, Duggan replied, "Bailey Youngson."

Later in the morning, Leadville law officers again questioned Mart Duggan, and this time he told them, "I don't know who shot me."

In disbelief, one of the officers asked, "What?"

Duggan's reply was, "Don't know who it was. Was one of the gang. I'll die before I tell you."

The officers pressed the issue, asking, "Was it Bailey Youngson?"

To this, Duggan said, "No!" It was also his last word as he slipped into a coma. The ex-marshal died at around 11:00 A.M., April 9, 1888. It was almost five years to the day since he had first walked the streets of Leadville wearing the badge of city marshal.

Bailey Youngson, his partner Jim Harrington, and faro dealer George Evans were arrested and charged with Duggan's murder. Since there was no real evidence against Harrington or Evans, they were released. Youngson was acquitted, again for lack of evidence. After George Evans died in 1902, the truth came out that he had been hired by some of Duggan's enemies to gun down the ex-marshal.

Louis Lamb's widow did deliver her "widow's weeds" to Mrs. Duggan as promised. She did not dance on Martin Duggan's grave, but danced in front of the Texas House where he had been shot.

Notes

1. Other accounts claim his pay was one hundred dollars a month in silver.

2. In G. W. Ratlett's 1903 article, "Mart Dougan [sic], Fighter," he says Duggan beat Rische with his gun so badly that it was feared Rische would die. There are errors in this article, however, which make Ratlett's reporting suspect.

References

Bartlett, G. W. "Mart Dougan [sic], Fighter." *The Rocky Mountain Magazine* 1, no. 10 (December 1903): 1.

Blair, Edward. *Leadville: Colorado's Magic City.* Boulder: Pruett Publishing Co., 1980, pp. 105-106, 111, 116-117, 120-122.

DeArment, Robert K. "Mart Duggan: Leadville Lawman." *Frontier Times* (February 1985): pp. 11-15.

Jessen, Kenneth. *Eccentric Colorado.* Boulder: Pruett Publishing Co., 1985, pp. 133-135.

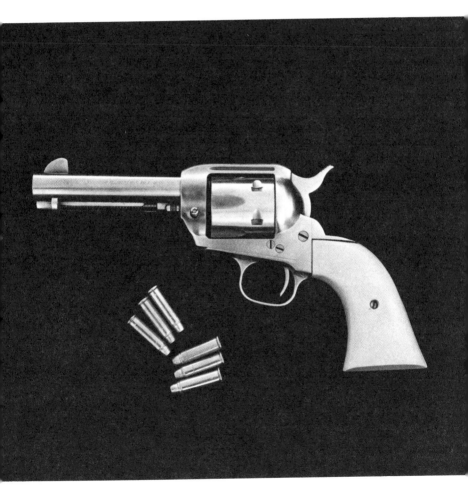

The Capture of the Allison Gang

C harles Ennis was employed as a waiter in one of the cheap boarding houses in Eureka, Nevada. While others got rich at mining, Charles worked for low wages and grew more and more resentful of the wealthy. Finally, in the early part of May 1879, he quit work and began planning to hold up the stagecoach that ran between Eureka and Ruby Hill. Ennis waited until payday at the mines; he knew the miners would be traveling down to Eureka to have some fun with their wages. In broad daylight, Charles Ennis and a partner held up the Eureka-bound stage and relieved its passengers of a month's hard-earned money plus whatever valuables they could take.

Following the robbery, Ennis and his partner took to the hills and reached Eureka about a half hour before the stage arrived. The two men immediately rode up to the livery stable door and began knocking. A voice from within answered, "What is it?"

Ennis replied, "Want to put up some horses."

The key turned, the door opened, and before the man inside could even open his mouth, a six-shooter was thrust into his face. Ennis warned, "Keep quiet or die!" The fellow was then tied and gagged. Another man was found asleep in the adjoining office, and he was also tied and gagged. An unlucky customer met the same fate.

The stage arrived at about eight o'clock that evening, and the passengers told the story of how they had been robbed. Practically the entire town came out as word spread quickly about the robbery. By acting totally unconcerned, Ennis and his partner made their way through the crowd on a pair of stolen horses and casually rode out of town.

In the meantime, one of the bound men in the livery stable worked himself free. He spread the word that the stagecoach robbers had just left town.

A posse was formed, and a man named Billy Martin was placed in charge of it. Martin tracked the outlaws through the night. Just after daybreak on the following morning, about forty miles northeast of Eureka, the eagle eyes of Billy Martin saw the fleeing culprits. He fired his gun into the air to signal his men to follow. Martin, mounted on a fast horse, gained quickly on Ennis and his companion. The robbers were forced to abandon their exhausted horses and run out into the dense brush in an attempt to hide from the persistent Martin.

Martin instructed his companions to keep riding at a moderate pace to lead the outlaws into believing that the posse had passed on by. He tied his horse to a clump of chaparral, took off his boots and hat, and began moving through the thorny brush on all fours. After about two hours of searching, he discovered Ennis and his companion crouched under a clump of brushweed. They were about fifty feet apart and some two hundred yards away. Martin approached the men as silently as an Indian until he was within pistol range. Quickly, he jumped to his feet and demanded that they surrender. Ennis immediately threw up his hands, but his companion drew and fired at Martin. He then began to run hard through the brush. Before he got ten steps, Martin put a bullet through his heart.

Billy Martin marched Ennis down to the thieves' horses and, as well as he could, tied him on top of one of them. By retracing his steps, Martin got his prisoner back to where he had left his own horse. A wagon was sent back to fetch the body of the dead bandit.

The prisoner was placed in the Eureka jail that evening, and his dead companion was buried in a pine box not far from the spot where the stage had been held up.

Prior to his involvement in the stage holdup, Charles Ennis had been well thought of in Eureka. He mingled well in society, rarely drank, and was quiet and gentlemanly. But unknown to the townspeople, he was wanted by the law in Chicago and was unable to claim the nearly ten thousand dollars he had inherited there. He was afraid of being arrested if he returned to Chicago.

In the Eureka jail, Ennis cried like a baby. He claimed his partner first gave him whiskey, then persuaded him to take part in the theft of the horses from the livery stable. He stoutly denied any knowledge of the stage robbery. The grand jury charged him with horse theft, but was forced to ignore the stage holdup for lack of evidence.

His behavior finally won the sympathy of the jailer. One evening, when the jailer went to lock him up for the night, Ennis begged to stay in the corridor outside his cell. He claimed he so sick to his stomach that he needed to reach the toilet frequently. The jailer had had no trouble with Ennis and decided to leave his cell open. He forgot about Ennis until around eleven o'clock that night. The jailer, intending to put Ennis back in his cell, unlocked the door leading to the corridor. He left the key in the lock and entered the corridor calling, "Ennis, Ennis." The sly outlaw was hidden behind the toilet door and quickly stepped out the corridor door. He closed the door behind him and locked the jailer inside. The embarrassed jailer was not found until the following morning.

It took the state law officers a lot of effort, but Charles Ennis was finally recaptured near the Utah line and brought back to Eureka. In the latter part of 1879, he was tried and convicted of horse theft and sentenced to eight years hard labor at the state prison in Carson City.

While en route to the prison over the Central Pacific Railway, Ennis slipped out of his irons. He was guarded by two law officers, but somehow momentarily distracted them. He jumped from the moving train, running at full speed to break his fall. Nevada law officers were unable to track him down a second time, and eventually he made his way to Colorado. Here he changed his name to Charles Allison.

Ironically, the outlaw made friends with Sheriff Joe Smith of Conejos County. The sheriff had no idea of his background. Ennis, alias Allison, was made deputy sheriff, the perfect cover for a fugitive. He executed his duties well but eventually drifted back into the holdup business while still a deputy sheriff. He picked up Lewis Perkins and Henry Watts as partners.

In the spring of 1881, Alamosa became the terminus of the Denver & Rio Grande Railroad. Stages met the trains and ran from there to other Colorado towns, such as Durango, Silverton, and Lake City. All of this stage traffic provided a fruitful field for Allison and his gang. In less than a month, they were credited with robbing five coaches.

Its success around Alamosa led the gang to expand its sphere of operation. The outlaws rode into Chama, New Mexico, firing their revolvers at anything that moved. The residents fled for their lives. The men then plundered the town at leisure by going through the stores, one by one, taking all the money they could find and any merchandise that met their fancy. A few days later, they shot up Pagosa Springs and were again rewarded with goods and cash.

One of the better-known lawmen in southern Colorado was Frank A. Hyatt of Alamosa. He was the assistant superintendent of the Rocky Mountain Detective Association for an area covering Arizona, New Mexico, and southern Colorado. Hyatt had the record for bringing in more criminals than any other law officer in this area.

The people of Colorado and New Mexico were fed up with the stage robberies and the ransacking of towns. As a result, Colorado Governor Pitkin offered $1,000 for the capture of Charles Allison and $250 each for his partners. New Mexico Governor Shelton added another $500 in reward money. The services of Frank Hyatt were sought, and a warrant was issued.

About that time, a local criminal by the name of Thomas Seeley, also known as "Tommy the Kid," was captured in Alamosa and placed in jail. He had information about the Allison gang and began talking. He tipped off Frank Hyatt that, after leaving Chama, Allison was most likely headed south toward Albuquerque. Tommy was later released for turning state's evidence.

Hyatt immediately secured the services of Hank Dorris, an old rancher; Miles Blaine, an Alamosa saloon keeper; and Cy Afton, a local painter. The four men set out after the Allison gang by boarding a narrow-gauge Denver & Rio Grande train and heading south. The line ended at Espanola, and the men switched to a stagecoach to travel to Santa Fe. From there they took another train to Albuquerque.

Hyatt felt sure the robbers would cross the Rio Grande River at Albuquerque, so he posted his men near the bridge leading into town. He then rode into town and inquired whether a trio answering the gang's description had been through. He concluded they had not reached Albuquerque and returned to inform his men. He then took a train to the small town of Bernalillo, about fifteen miles north on the road to Santa Fe.

In the morning Detective Hyatt decided to get a bite to eat. While he was eating, who should walk in but Charles Allison, Lewis Perkins, and Henry Watts. They propped their Winchesters by the door and ordered some food. It was a tense situation, since Hyatt had met Allison when they were both serving as deputy sheriffs of Conejos County. Had the detective given the slightest sign he recognized Allison, he would probably have been shot on the spot. Instead, Hyatt's face remained emotionless, and as the gang entered, he simply looked up momentarily and said, "Good morning, gentlemen," then continued eating his meal.

When Hyatt finished breakfast, he walked out of the cafe, maintaining a casual manner. As soon as he was out of sight, he hurried to the railroad depot and telegraphed Hank Dorris to gather up Blaine and Afton and ride north. Hyatt watched the Allison gang ride off to the south. He tried to purchase a horse, but couldn't find a single animal for sale. Finally, an old Mexican drove into town with two fine horses hitched to a wagon. After some bargaining, Hyatt agreed to pay the exorbitant price of one hundred dollars for one of the animals if the Mexican would ride with him. The pair immediately set out after the outlaws.

Hyatt stayed out of sight as he tracked the gang. Charles Allison and his men stopped about two miles from Albuquerque and made camp. The detective looked in the distance toward Albuquerque for his men but could see no sign of them. The only thing he could do was to cut across toward town with his Mexican partner. They found the posse just saddling their horses. Apparently it had taken a while for the telegraph to reach them.

Hyatt knew that if he tried to capture the Allison gang at their camp there would be a shootout. The operator of the livery stable, Jeff Grant, volunteered to ride out to Allison's camp and try to lure the outlaws into town. He rode bareback, pretending to be looking for stray horses, and boldly rode right into their camp. He asked if the men had spotted any strays in the area. During the conversation, Allison told Grant that the gang was headed to Lincoln County, New Mexico. Grant pretended to like this idea and said he also needed to go down there in a few days with some money to deliver a string of racehorses. He asked the men to delay their trip and accompany him because the country was infested with thieves. He also told the men he was in the livery business and that they were welcome to rest their weary horses for free in his stable. The outlaws were tempted by Grant's offer. After all, they could rest their animals at someone else's expense, then rob that same person of his money and horses on their way to Lincoln County.

Meanwhile, back at the livery stable, Hyatt and his men waited. Soon they could see Allison, Grant, and the rest of the gang riding toward town. The posse hid in Grant's barn. Hyatt climbed up into the hayloft, while the others hid in the stables. The gang rode right into the barn and dismounted. Grant led their horses away.

The three outlaws stood close together, not suspecting a thing. The time was right. Hyatt yelled, "Throw up your hands!" The men hesitated for a moment until they saw the gleam of a Winchester only a few feet from their heads. Three pairs of hands reached for the sky. The men were disarmed, taken to a local blacksmith shop, and placed in irons.[1]

Perkins and Watts were thoroughly disheartened by their arrest. Allison remained quite cheerful, but he feared that the worst was yet to come when he was returned to Colorado and his real name and background were discovered.

A local law officer by the name of D. I. Sullivan demanded that Hyatt turn over his prisoners. Hyatt refused, but was forced to give up his reward from the state of New Mexico as a compromise.

Hyatt, his men, and the prisoners returned to Alamosa. Suffering from exhaustion and loss of sleep, Hyatt went home to bed, but in a few minutes he was awakened by a messenger, sent by Mayor Broadwell, telling him that a lynch mob had formed. The detective gathered some of his most trusted friends and removed the prisoners from jail. The mob had arranged to have a caboose and locomotive ready to pull out of town so they could lynch the Allison gang without interference from the local authorities. The plan backfired when Hyatt managed to get Allison and his men to the caboose first. The train pulled out, leaving the lynch mob behind.

On June 25, 1881, the day following the escape from the lynch mob, the Allison gang was placed safely behind the bars of the Arapahoe County jail in Denver. Governor Pitkin tendered the fifteen hundred dollar reward to Hyatt, adding an additional fifty dollars out of his own pocket.

After the excitement had subsided, the three outlaws were returned to Conejos County to stand trial. They were convicted and sentenced to the state penitentiary for thirty-seven years. Lewis Perkins was pardoned after serving eight years. He ended up running a saloon and gambling hall in Trinidad, and he became fairly wealthy in the process. Charles Ennis, alias Charles Allison, was pardoned after ten years. He moved to Butte, Montana, where he changed his name once again and took a job as a bartender. Henry Watts was pardoned along with Ennis, only to join a band of train robbers in Arizona. He was killed in 1895.

Notes

1. In the June 18, 1881, issue of the *Rocky Mountain News*, the story of the capture of the Allison gang is quite different. Local law officer D. I. Sullivan was said to have pulled his revolver and demanded the surrender of the gang in the livery stable. The gang was covered by "twenty revolvers in the hands of twenty men . . . in the stalls of the stable." Grant and Sullivan claimed the reward money. The governor of New Mexico told Sullivan to hold the gang in jail until the matter of who had jurisdiction over the prisoners could be cleared up by the adjutant general of the territory.

References

"The Allison Gang." *The Rocky Mountain News,* June 26, 1881.

"Allison Gang Captured." *The Colorado Prospector* 5, no. 6 (June 1974): 4, 6.

"Allison History." *The Rocky Mountain News,* June 19, 1881.

"Caught at Albuquerque." *The Rocky Mountain News,* June 18, 1881.

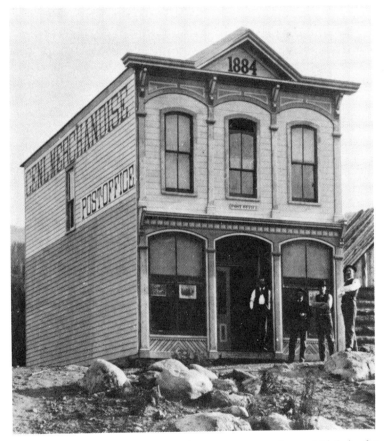

Grand Lake was a rough and tumble western town located high in the Colorado Rocky Mountains. During the 1880s, its main industry was mining and lumber. Pictured here is the Grand Lake post office and general store on the town's main street. *Grand County Museum*

County Commissioners Ambushed at Grand Lake

It was a fine day in the Colorado Rockies. Grand Lake was like a mirror, reflecting the dense forest and snow-capped peaks across its expanse. The only element to disturb this tranquil setting was the occasional popping of Independence Day firecrackers. It was 1883, and a fledging tourist business struggled to establish itself in the mining economy of the town of Grand Lake. Any human would have found peace in this magnificent setting. Young children played on the rocks at the water's edge. The sun's warmth was just beginning to take the chill off the morning.

No one noticed a small group of men assembled behind a small hill near the shore. One of these men was Grand County Commissioner John Gillis Mills; two others were Undersheriff William Redman and his brother, Mann; and the fourth member of the party was the sheriff of Grand County, Charles Royer. All of the men wore holstered revolvers, but Commissioner Mills also carried a Sharps carbine. Behind some of the glacial boulders deposited during the last ice age, the men put on roughly fashioned masks made from common sackcloth. Their horses were tethered in a clump of dense lodgepole pine.

Mills, the leader of the group, had specific and violent plans for the other two Grand County commissioners. The Redman brothers relished any sort of excitement. Sheriff Royer, however, thought that the mission was just to scare the other two commissioners.

Meanwhile, at the Fairview House, run by Mrs. Mary Young, county commissioners Barney Day and Edward P. Weber were having a leisurely breakfast with County Clerk Thomas J. "Cap" Dean. They discussed fishing, and it was well past eight o'clock before the three men departed on foot to attend the next commissioners session at the Grand County courthouse in Grand Lake. Barney Day brought along a loaded .45-caliber revolver out of habit. Dean always carried a Colt Navy model revolver. Weber was unarmed and had only a bundle of papers.

The three men strolled abreast along a wagon road leading from the Fairview House back toward the town. As they passed between some boulders amid a dense stand of trees and a log structure used as an icehouse, they were ambushed. A report rang out, and Weber stiffened and gasped, "Oh! . . . I'm shot!" The slug had entered his back below the right shoulder and passed entirely through his body. Day and Dean eased their wounded companion to the ground. A group of masked men emerged from behind the boulders. Their leader carried a smoking Sharps carbine.

Cap Dean found himself staring down the barrels of two revolvers. He jumped aside and drew his revolver, but one of the masked men fired first. The ball smashed into the bridge of his nose. He reeled away, blinded in one eye, and tried to run for cover. Another shot was fired and the ball entered the back of Dean's hip and came out the front, splintering his pelvis and dropping him immediately. The masked man with the carbine began an unmerciful beating of the wounded man.

Barney Day, experienced at using firearms, got off several shots. The first, delivered at point-blank range, went into the rifleman's head. The ball entered behind his ear and passed through his brain, killing him instantly. Day ran back behind the icehouse, but two of the masked men surrounded the structure. As Day came around the south side, he met one of the men. He fired quickly, breaking the man's right arm and knocking the gun out of his hand. As Day turned to meet his other attacker, he was shot through the heart; he stumbled a few steps and fell headlong into the lake.

The shots had been mixed with the 4th of July fireworks. Dean was in shock but remained conscious. He kept still, fearing that one of the masked men would issue a coup de grace. Brain matter oozed from the ragged hole behind the ear of the dead rifleman. Day lay half-submerged in the cold lake, his blood mixing with the clear water. He was dead. Weber, with a bullet through his lungs, struggled to his feet and tried to make it back to the Fairview. He collapsed, hemorrhaging badly.

By the time anyone reached the victims, Weber had lapsed into unconsciousness, and the papers in his pocket were soaked with blood. Dean somehow managed to stagger toward the

The Fairview House was where county commissioners Barney Day and E. P. Weber, along with T. J. "Cap" Dean, enjoyed a leisurely breakfast on July 4, 1883, before being ambushed in Grand Lake, Colorado. After the shooting, proprietress Mary Young allowed two of the badly wounded men to be brought into her establishment. Although she scrubbed the floors repeatedly, she was unable to remove the bloodstains. *Grand County Museum*

Fairview and was helped in. Weber was carried inside. Mrs. Young did her best to comfort the wounded men. An attempt was made to find Sheriff Royer or Undersheriff Redman, but the citizens of Grand Lake had no way of knowing that these men took part in the shooting.

Max James pushed his way through the onlookers to the body of the masked rifleman. After turning the body over, James tore off the powder-burned mask and revealed the face of Commissioner John Mills. James was sympathetic to Weber's side of a dispute involving the location of the county seat, the dispute that had precipitated the ambush, and commented, "The Goddamned son of a bitch should have been killed long ago." Evidence was gathered, including Day's revolver with four of its six chambers fired; Dean's revolver, which had not been fired; and Mills's rifle, which had been fired once. Of interest was a trail of splattered blood leading away from the icehouse for a distance of nearly a quarter mile. The wounded man had evidently been helped onto his horse at the end of the trail of blood.

It took only a few hours before an inquest was conducted. The six-man jury, hastily assembled from those who were available, found that the "deceased had come to their deaths at the hands of some unknown persons in a felonious manner." It seemed a rather odd verdict, since Mills was clearly identified and had taken part in the shooting.

A doctor from the mining town of Teller looked at Weber and proclaimed his condition hopeless. Weber died the next morning, bringing the death toll in the shooting to three.

Dean appeared to be fully alert despite the serious wounds he had suffered, and he was able to provide a bedside deposition of what had happened. His head wound was extraordinary. The ball had penetrated the bridge of his nose and had passed to the back of his skull without affecting his mental functions. The ball, however, could not be removed. His hip had been shattered by the second shot. The doctor believed there was no way to prevent infection in such a massive wound. Dean knew the truth about his condition and conveyed most of his property to his son Fred. By July 13, there was unmistakable evidence of infection in the hip. Two days later, Dean lapsed into unconsciousness, and on July 17, he died.

Mills was buried in the Grand Lake cemetery, and Day and Dean were buried at Hot Sulphur Springs. Weber was given what was to be a temporary burial on his ranch. His wife sold the place soon after, but the body was never removed to a formal cemetery.

The four deaths did not end the trouble in Grand County, Colorado. Sheriff Charles Royer, widely admired, had been on duty at Grand Lake at noon that July 4. After taking part in the shooting, he suddenly appeared in Hot Sulphur Springs that afternoon. He was nervous and insisted that all was fine in Grand Lake and that the county commissioners were in a meeting. A short time later, a rider from Grand Lake spread the word about the shooting. Royer fell into a state of utter confusion. The citizens of Hot Sulphur Springs, who had been looking forward to a wonderful July 4th celebration, were stunned and outraged at the news. Royer pleaded in despair, "What can I do? I don't know who to go after."

Even before the shootings, residents of Grand Lake and Hot Sulphur Springs had not been on good terms because of the conflict over the location of the county seat; they half expected to be assaulted by war parties from the opposing town. A message was dispatched from the closest telegraph office on the other side of the Continental Divide requesting the militia be sent to restore law and order. The telegram was delivered directly to Colorado's Governor James B. Grant a little past midnight on July 5. The militia was not sent. Confusion spread through Denver since the story could not be easily confirmed because of the remoteness of Grand County. Rumors were fabricated to fill space, and soon the newspapers accused Hot Sulphur Springs of sending a masked mob against the people of Grand Lake. It was even rumored that the governor was considering a special session of the legislature to wipe Grand County from the map!

Sheriff Royer was unable to explain why he had not been able to find the culprits nor why a posse wasn't formed. He also had been seen in the company of Undersheriff Redman leaving the scene of the shooting, with the two of them on horses.

After a few days, Royer fled to Georgetown, on the other side of Berthoud Pass. He took a room in the Ennis House on Taos Street. Late in the afternoon of the following day, he was found sprawled on the floor of the hotel room. His head rested in a

After the shooting in Grand Lake, Sheriff Charles Royer fled over Berthoud Pass to Georgetown and stayed at the Ennis House, shown in this photograph. Royer confessed his involvement in the shooting to a close friend before committing suicide in his hotel room. The friend kept the confession a secret for several years. *Loveland Public Library*

pool of clotted blood. His revolver lay by his feet, bringing the deaths stemming from the gunfight to five. An inquest in Georgetown produced a verdict of suicide. At the time, no one had any idea that Royer was involved in the incident, and it was believed he had crumpled under the heavy criticism of how he had handled the case. Others believed he could not face arresting his friend, Bill Redman. Shortly before his suicide, Royer confessed his crime to a close friend, who held it secret for several years.

A great deal of mystery surrounds the fate of Bill Redman. On August 7, a group of cowboys was following some cattle near the Ouray Indian Agency in southwestern Colorado. They found a man lying dead in the grass. The cowboys assumed the man had been murdered and his body left to rot on the plains. They returned to the agency and reported their discovery to Major J. F. Minniss. The next day, Major Minniss returned to the location with a half-dozen Indians from the agency to give the man a decent burial.

While Minniss was searching the victim's pockets for some identification, one of the Indians found some marks traced in the sand alongside the trail: someone had written the name "William Redman" in large, clear letters. What puzzled the major was who wrote it: the murderer or the victim? Next, a saddle was found a short distance away with "William Redman, Middle Park, Colorado" scratched on it.

If the murderer had desired to remove all evidence of his crime, he would hardly have written the name of his victim in the sand and left the saddle nearby. Also there was fifty dollars cash on the body. When the body was turned over, a Colt revolver was found. It had been fired once. There was a wound above the left eye that showed where the ball had penetrated the brain. The major changed his analysis, now believing the body to be Redman's and that he had committed suicide.

Others say that Redman was sheltered by his wife after the shooting until his wound healed sufficiently for him to travel. They say Redman escaped the law forever by then killing an innocent man and putting the body along the trail.

"Squeaky" Bob Wheeler, a well-known Grand County resident, claimed that Bill Redman escaped to Arizona after his involvement in the Grand Lake shooting and became head of a

Bill Redman was undersheriff at the time of the shooting in Grand Lake, Colorado, in 1883, and it is almost certain he and his brother were involved in the ambush that cost four men their lives. The shooting involved a dispute over the location of the county seat, and during the incident, Redman was badly wounded. He subsequently disappeared. *Grand County Museum*

gang of outlaws. Wheeler said he saw Redman in the flesh, in a small Wyoming town, years after the shooting.

But why did the shooting take place? These acts of violence were the culmination of a long-festering feud in Grand County over the location of the county seat. Hot Sulphur Springs, located on the road over Berthoud Pass and the center for ranching in the area, had been the logical center of Grand County. But by 1880, the economic focus had shifted to the town of Grand Lake and its mines. A petition sent to the county commissioners and signed by eighty-one residents of Grand Lake asked for a special election to be held in the summer of 1880. Hot Sulphur Springs managed to get the date set back to November 2, 1880.

By a margin of 114 to 83, Grand Lake won the popular vote for county seat, but the issue didn't die. The Board of Canvassers (predominantly from Hot Sulphur Springs) managed to disallow enough ballots to adjust the outcome in Hot Sulphur Springs's favor. Grand Lakers were furious, and to make matters worse, Colorado state law would not allow another vote on the issue for four years.

On April 9, 1881, the recently seated Board of Commissioners moved to adjust matters. The new board reflected the mining interests in Grand Lake and was led by John Gillis Mills. Using his power, Mills announced that the canvassers had exceeded their legal rights and had falsified returns. Grand Lake was then declared the legal and proper county seat. All county offices were directed to move to Grand Lake. Hilary Harris, the sole commissioner from Hot Sulphur Springs, was helpless to change their decision. Soon, a $350 courthouse was built in Grand Lake, along with a sturdy jail.

Hot Sulphur Springs had not given up, however, and William N. Byers, former editor of the *Rocky Mountain News* in Denver, along with Thomas J. "Cap" Dean, fought the move. Dean carried his arguments to the district court, with Edward P. Weber acting as the principal attorney. Eventually, Dean, counseled by Weber and subsidized by Byers, took the issue of the location of the county seat all the way to the Colorado Supreme Court. In April 1882, the matter was tossed back to the district court in Grand Lake. The judge found in favor of Grand Lake. Hot Sulphur Springs aquiesced, but its seeming surrender was only superficial.

Mills, who lived in the mining town of Teller, continued to push for more road improvements, which favored the mining industry. He got into a quarrel with town officials in Teller and turned toward Grand Lake for help with road improvements.

Mills's runaway spending on roads got the county into serious trouble. During the last half of 1881, the county spent $7,957 against receipts of only $2,348, and by the end of the year, the indebtedness grew to $12,000. Most of the debt was carried in warrants at a 10 percent interest rate on their face value. Grand County warrants were considered so risky that Denver investors were only willing to pay 65 cents on the dollar for them.

To increase his power, Mills formed an alliance with William A. Hamill, a wealthy Georgetown mine owner and an Englishman by birth. Hamill was always well dressed and impeccably manicured; he was also a little overweight and did not fit into frontier society. Neverthess, his ability to manage, combined with his great wealth, made him a prominent figure. After Hamill declared that he had Grand County in his "vest pocket," indignation swept the area, and Weber formed his own alliance with "Cap" Dean. The *Grand Lake Prospector,* a newspaper some say was founded to serve Mills's interests, hurled editorial bombs at Weber and Dean using the words "thief," "small-brain," "miserable sneak," and "cowardly tool."

The winter of 1882–1883 came early and hard. Grand Lake bustled with activity, including an all-night ball. The morning after the ball, a drunken altercation occurred between Wilson Waldern and his wife. Waldern was a county commissioner who was just about to retire. H. B. Rogerson replaced Waldern, but could not raise the bond money for the office. Edward P. Weber was picked by the governor to replace Rogerson. Mills was now pitted against his worst enemy, Weber. As Weber began to dominate the commission, Mills plotted to kill Weber, Day, and Dean.

After the July 4 shooting and the loss of the entire board of commissioners, emergency action was necessary. Mills, Weber, and Day had to be replaced. It would have been understandable if no one were willing to serve, but much to the surprise of many, several applications were waiting on the governor's desk within forty-eight hours of the incident. The governor carefully avoided individuals polarized toward either faction. The new

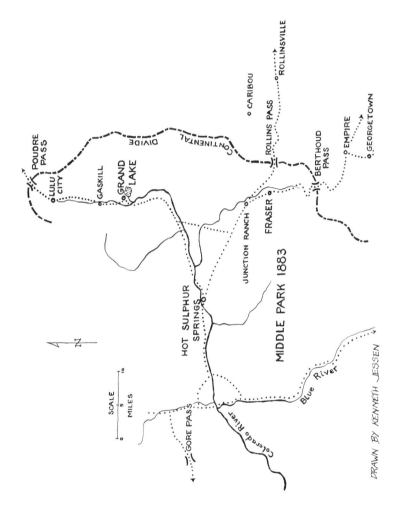

MIDDLE PARK 1883

POUDRE PASS
LULU CITY
GASKILL
GRAND LAKE
CONTINENTAL DIVIDE
CARIBOU
ROLLINS PASS
ROLLINSVILLE
BERTHOUD PASS
EMPIRE
GEORGETOWN
FRASER
JUNCTION RANCH
HOT SULPHUR SPRINGS
GORE PASS
Colorado River
Blue River

N

SCALE
MILES
0   5   10

DRAWN BY KENNETH JESSEN

commissioners met for four days to try to put Grand County back in order, to pay all bills, and to appoint a new sheriff.

Trying to find out who murdered Dean and Day was not easy. Bill Redman had vanished or had committed suicide. Royer was dead. Alonzo Coffin and J. Gilman Martin were supposedly in on the plot, and on August 20, 1883, at the regular session of the district court, these two men and Bill Redman were charged with murder. Coffin and Martin were arraigned, pleaded not guilty, and were released on bond. It turned out that a local surveyor who supplied damaging testimony to the grand jury was drunk when he made his statements. When the case came to trial, the state's two witnesses had disappeared. The men were found not guilty and were released.

Ironically, in 1888, the county seat was moved back to Hot Sulphur Springs.

References

Black, Robert C. III. *Island in the Rockies.* Boulder: Pruett Publishing Co., 1969, pp. 167-228.

Cairns, Mary Lyons. *Grand Lake: The Pioneers.* Denver: The World Press, Inc. 1946, pp. 221-237.

"The Contending Factions Meet at Grand Lake; Masks, Pistols and Death." Georgetown *Colorado Miner,* July 7, 1883.

"Denver Reporters Fail to get Correct Story, Cap Dean's Full Story is Told Here." Georgetown *Colorado Miner,* July 14, 1883.

"Former Commissioner Murders Mine Foreman." Georgetown *Colorado Miner,* January 27, 1883.

"Redmon's [sic] Remains Found." Georgetown *Colorado Miner,* October 6, 1883.

"Serious Trouble is Brewing." Georgetown *Colorado Miner,* June 16, 1883.

"Sheriff Royer Kills Self." Georgetown *Colorado Miner,* July 21, 1883.

This photograph of Hot Sulphur Springs, located along the Colorado River, shows the town in its early days. It was founded as a health spa by the editor of the *Rocky Mountain News*, William Byers. *Colorado Historical Society*

Hot Sulphur Springs Exterminates Texas Charley

C harles W. Wilson was a delinquent teenager who arrived in Middle Park in the spring of 1883. It is said he was from New Mexico or possibly Texas, but no one was sure.

Texas Charley, as he was known locally, labeled anyone he didn't like as a "son of a bitch." After he had spent a year and a half in Grand County, most of the prominent citizens fell into this category. Charley earned his keep working on the area's ranches. Between jobs he enjoyed long periods of idleness, which provided him the freedom to harass others. Along with other weapons, he carried two revolvers. He used them to entertain the clientele of various saloons by shooting between the legs of selected victims. He dressed in the late nineteenth century style of the American West, wearing a large sombrero. His two friends, J. V. Thompson and J. H. Caltharp, stuck close by Texas Charley. To the respectable citizens of the area, Texas Charley was becoming progressively more obnoxious.

The teenager frequented the saloons in Hot Sulphur Springs. It was there that Texas Charley, Thompson, and Caltharp came one Friday evening, December 5, 1884. Charley was intent on taking over the town for his own amusement, and his first target was Ute Bill's saloon. Charley leveled a revolver at the proprietor and demanded the shotgun that was kept behind the bar. Ute Bill was taken by surprise and had to surrender his firearm.

Texas Charley and his companions then moved on to the center of winter activity in Hot Sulphur Springs, the general store operated by Frank Byers and Frank Newton Briggs. A fellow by the name of W. L. Veatch became Charley's first victim there. He beat the man with the barrel of his revolver, then cocked the weapon and threatened to shoot Veatch right on the spot. Onlookers were kept at bay by the cocked revolver in the hands of J. V. Thompson.

After Texas Charley and his friends finished terrorizing Veatch, they left the store. Veatch immediately went to the justice of the peace, Calvin Kinney. But he demanded no legal action, just Kinney's gun! The justice refused to hand it over, and Veatch had to settle for swearing out a complaint.

Before the justice could finish drawing up the warrant, Charley stormed into the office, saying he wished to give up and be fined. The justice insisted that the warrant be completed first; this infuriated Texas Charley, and he threatened Kinney with one of his revolvers. Charley swore that if the warrant were ever served on him, he would seek out and kill everyone in the room. The justice held fast and Texas Charley walked out into the street and boasted that there were not enough real men in the town of Hot Sulphur Springs to arrest him. It soon became apparent that the town's local law officer, Constable William Patterson, was reluctant to undertake his duty and tangle with Charley. A transient was asked to deliver the warrant to Patterson, but Texas Charley intercepted it and tore it to shreds.

By December 9, Hot Sulphur Springs had had enough of Texas Charley, and another warrant was drawn up. Charley was informed that the warrant was on its way, but he seemed unconcerned. After all, he believed he was in control of the town. Nevertheless, when Charley and his cronies rode a buckboard that carried the U.S. mail from the outlying ranches into town that day, they stopped fifteen-year-old John Gardner on his way home from school and asked the boy if he thought Charley would be arrested when he reached town. John didn't know, but Charley and his friends Caltharp and Thompson loaded and checked their revolvers.

When the wagon reached the general store, Charley helped carry in the sack of mail. He and his partners then walked up the main street of Hot Sulphur Springs toward the Kinney House, where the justice of the peace held his sessions. Charley wore a single .45-caliber revolver with a bone handle. Part of the way up the street he pulled aside a fellow and told him that he might have to use his gun on Constable Patterson and W. L. Veatch.

Near the end of the street and close to the Kinney House was an abandoned store. Diagonally opposite the store stood "Doc" Bock's store, which was leased to a carpenter. When Texas Charley and his companions reached the space between the

"Doc" Bock's store is pictured above. It was from a window in this store that the citizens of Hot Sulphur Springs took the law into their own hands and gunned down Texas Charley. *Grand County Museum*

buildings, a gunshot rang out. The shot missed the men, and Caltharp and Thompson drew their weapons. Texas Charley remained cool and remarked, "Seems to be getting pretty warm around here." He had just pulled out his .45-caliber revolver when a second shot rang out. The bullet pierced Texas Charley's right hand, the hand holding the gun. He reacted by shifting the revolver to his left hand. Before he could locate his enemies and return the fire, however, a volley of shots rang out in the thin mountain air. Texas Charley Wilson slumped to the ground and lay still. Gunsmoke drifted from an open window in "Doc" Bock's store.

Fifteen men, bearing an assortment of guns, entered the street from the store to examine their prostrate target. All were prominent citizens of Hot Sulphur Springs. Texas Charley was dead from a full load of buckshot in the chest and a ball that had shattered his skull.

The body was carried into the carpentry shop. The store owner, "Doc" Bock, just happened to be the county coroner. An immediate inquest was held, and a jury was empaneled from the bystanders, with Charley's corpse laid out in front of them. Although a number of witnesses were questioned, their memories unaccountably failed them, and none could recall the identity of any of the assassins. Although a high percentage of Hot Sulphur Springs residents were involved in the killing, the verdict of the jury after questioning the witnesses was, "We . . . find that said C. W. Wilson came to his death by gunshot wounds at the hands of some person or persons to us unknown."

The corpse yielded little information about Texas Charley. The bone-handled .45-caliber revolver had not been fired. Charley was carrying a renewal notice for his subscription to the *Colfax County Stockman*. A well-worn letter to a Charles McMahon from his wife was discovered. No connection could be found to McMahon. There were a few pornographic postcards, an engraved request for a lady's permission to escort her home, and a Denver pawnbroker's card. Finally, Charley had a printed saloon ticket that read, "Good for one drink, T. J. D." The initials T. J. D. stood for a local saloon owner, Thomas J. Dean, killed earlier in a shootout at Grand Lake. (See chapter 14, "County Commissioners Ambushed at Grand Lake.")

The newspapers generally approved of the method used to eliminate Wilson. The *Rocky Mountain News* termed him "a public enemy, a beastly enemy to man" and went on to conclude that those who killed him were "public benefactors."

References

Black, Robert C. *Island in the Rockies.* Boulder: Pruett Publishing Co., 1969, pp. 220-224.

Scott, Jay. "Who Killed Texas Charley?" *True Western Adventures* (February 1961): 13.

Gunnison's famous sheriff Cyrus Wells "Doc" Shores spent many years
tracking down criminals and, in the process, became one of Colorado's
most effective law officers. He is shown here in 1927 with his
stenographer, Helda Swansen. Doc Shores died in 1934 at the age of
ninety. *Colorado Historical Society*

Doc Shores
Captures
Train Robbers

A Denver & Rio Grande passenger train left Grand Junction early on the morning of November 3, 1887. It had come from Salt Lake City and was headed east. At around 3:45 A.M., at a point five miles east of Grand Junction, the engineer saw a pile of rocks across the tracks just ahead on a sharp curve at Unaweep Switch along the Gunnison River. The engineer applied the brakes and brought the train to a jolting stop. As he did so, four masked men appeared out of the darkness. They were armed and ordered the engineer and fireman down from the locomotive cab. One of the train robbers covered the two trainmen and forced them to hold their hands in the air.

The other three robbers then walked down to the mail car and pounded on the door, shouting, "Open up." Mail clerk H. W. Grubb was fast asleep. When he heard the noise, he jumped up, believing the train had arrived in Delta. With the Delta mail pouch in hand, he opened the door. As the crisp November air began to fill the warm car, he was astonished to see three masked men standing before him. One of them held a rifle, and the other two had revolvers. The important fact was that all of the guns were pointed at him. He could see the fourth bandit off in the darkness, keeping his six-shooter trained on the engineer and fireman.

One of the masked men commanded, "Put up your hands and get out of the car."

The mail clerk dropped the pouch and jumped to the ground.

The robber asked, "Is anyone else inside the mail car?"

"No. I was all alone," replied Grubb.

"Then get back inside and stand up against the wall with your face toward it," the robber insisted, keeping his gun trained on the mail clerk.

As Grubb climbed over the door sill and back into the car, the three train robbers followed. They rifled the mail pouches and set aside all registered letters and packages. The clerk stood at the end of the car with his hands raised.

Grubb pleaded, "Gentlemen, it's gettin' awful cold in here and I've been coming down with the grippe. Would you mind if I got my coat?"

He was allowed to put on his coat and was reminded at gunpoint not to try any tricks. After a few minutes, Grubb was ordered out of the car again and was kept covered, along with the engineer and fireman.

The outlaws left the mail car and walked down to the express car. One of them hammered on the locked door, calling for the express agent to open up. The agent, Dick Williams, had guessed what was going on when the train came to an unscheduled stop. He carried a revolver and also had a shotgun in the car. He refused to open the door, saying that there were trunks piled against it and that they should go around to the other side of the car. He tried to get a look at the robbers to determine if he could defend the car, but it was too dark. When the train robbers threatened to blow the car up with dynamite, Williams decided that discretion was the better part of valor and opened the door. Besides, there was precious little to steal.

There were two safes in the express car, and Williams was told to open them. One safe was a messenger's safe, which Williams quickly opened. It yielded about $150, which hardly satisfied the robbers. Williams was given just three minutes to open the other, larger, safe, which was the "through safe" belonging to the express company. He pleaded with the bandits, telling them that its combination was known only by station agents along the line. One of the marked men pulled out his watch and said, "I mean business." He continued to point his revolver at the express agent. "If that safe ain't opened in three minutes, I'm going to blow your head off."

Williams continued his appeal, saying, "Can't you understand that I don't know how to open it? We messengers are not allowed to have the combination to the through safe. It is known only to the agents at the more important depots."

"Quit stallin'. Your time is running out," the robber threatened as he glanced at his watch.

The mail clerk continued to plead, "If you let me get in my coat, I'll show you a letter from the general manager of the express company proving that I am not authorized to know the combination." The agent frantically searched through his pockets, but was unable to produce the letter. Glancing at his watch, the robber reminded Williams that he had thirty seconds left to live.

Williams now expected to be shot dead and could hear the final seconds ticking away. Finally the silence was broken by, "Time's up!"

As the masked man pocketed his watch, one of his companions asked, "Shall I let him have it?" He raised his revolver so that it pointed right at the express agent's head.

The answer was, "No, let him go. I believe he's tellin' the truth."

The masked men removed a three-pound express package and a few envelopes marked C.O.D. They pocketed the cash from the messenger safe, then forced Williams to stand with his hands up, along with the mail clerk, engineer, and fireman. The robbers returned to the mail car and ransacked it a second time, leaving letters scattered on the floor.

At that point, the brakeman and a passenger started walking up toward the locomotive to see why the train had stopped. The masked guard fired two warning shots at them and drove them back inside the passenger car.

It was a chilly November night, and the railroad men were growing tired of holding their hands in the air. The fireman was the first to complain. "My arms are getting too tired to hold up much longer," he said. "May I lower them for a moment?"

The guard said, "Lock your fingers together and place your hands on the top of your head. That will help. The rest of you may do the same."

The robbers considered going through the coach and pullman car to rob the passengers, as they had found only the $150 in the safe and a few express packages of unknown value. Remembering that shots had been fired at the brakeman and one passenger, however, they had second thoughts. They feared that some of the passengers might be armed and ready to fight.

In fact, the conductor had awakened all the passengers and informed them of what was happening. He tried to keep everyone calm, telling them the holdup men were most likely only after express packages and mail. A young Scotchman, however, became so frightened that he grabbed some clothing from a female passenger. He quickly put on the clothing, trying to disguise himself. The conductor quieted him down and returned the garments to their owner.

Nevertheless, the train robbers departed into the darkness, and after removal of the rock across the track, the journey to Delta was completed. When dawn came, word of the daring holdup spread rapidly through the area. The famous Gunnison sheriff Cyrus Wells "Doc" Shores was called in to solve the case. As an inducement, a four thousand dollar reward was offered (worth more than forty thousand dollars in today's money). Doc Shores selected his brother-in-law, M. L. Allison, as his partner. Allison just happened to be visiting his sister and was not an experienced law officer.

The two men took the train that had been held up toward Delta. When the engineer pulled to a stop at Kanna Creek, about ten miles from the holdup site, Sheriff Shores and M. L. Allison climbed into the cab. The trainmen were the same men who were on duty the night of the holdup. This, in fact, was their first trip over the line since the holdup. As the engineer approached Unaweep Switch, he appeared tense and jumpy, even with Doc Shores in the cab. As he neared the scene of the crime, he sailed on by, then finally applied the brakes. Shores and Allison got off and were forced to walk back to the switch.

As soon as it was light, the two men began searching for clues. Doc Shores knew holdup men frequently used tobacco and often left matches, cigarette butts, or tobacco plugs on the ground because of the nervous tension involved in committing a crime, especially one as spectacular as a train robbery. All such evidence, however, had been obliterated by the tracks of many men on horseback. A Mesa County posse had beaten them to the scene of the crime.

The railroad ran along the north bank of the Gunnison River all the way to Delta. To the north, the ground was steep and rocky, making travel difficult. Using his methodical approach to tracking criminals, Shores first walked several miles along the railroad tracks toward Grand Junction along with Allison. The men then circled north and back to the railroad tracks a number of miles above Unaweep Switch. Although the ground wasn't cluttered by the tracks of the posse, the two men saw no sign of the robbers. During the rest of the day, Shores and Allison continued to make ever wider circles north of the railroad. Still no sign could be found of the robbers. They couldn't find any evidence that the robbers had walked any great distance from the holdup site along the riverbank either. The only route of escape was across the Gunnison River.

Shores and Allison went to Grand Junction to spend the night. Using rented saddle horses, the two men started out early the next morning to continue the search. They crossed the Gunnison on a ferry and rode slowly along the south bank of the river looking for tracks. By nightfall, no signs had been found, so the weary men returned to their Grand Junction hotel.

With fresh horses, they set out once again the next day. They again crossed the river and returned to the point where they had stopped their search the previous day. After traveling less than a mile beyond Unaweep Switch, they noticed fresh footprints made by a man walking up from the river. He had left deep tracks in the mud. Shores took a closer look at the tracks and noticed that the prints were actually made by two men, one walking directly behind the other. The tracks led toward Bangs Canyon.

Shores and Allison followed the prints for a while, but then returned to the river to look for the tracks of the other two robbers. After crossing Bangs Canyon about a mile above Unaweep Switch, Shores found the fresh footprints of the other two men. They were headed southwest in the same general direction as the first set of tracks.

Bangs Canyon had no trail in it and ran from the Gunnison River southwest up onto a high plateau with elevations above 9,000 feet. The canyon paralleled Unaweep Canyon but was not nearly as deep. A wagon road ran up Unaweep Canyon over to Paradox Valley. Bangs Canyon was a logical escape route in that it ended in a very remote area.

After spending another night in Grand Junction, Shores and Allison again set out on saddle horses toward Bangs Canyon. They picked up one set of tracks. After heading southwest for several miles, the tracks dropped into the canyon. This forced Shores and Allison to dismount and lead their horses down the rocky canyon walls. At this point, they were about fourteen miles from the river. Before they had gone very far, the tracks of the other two outlaws joined those of their comrades. The trail now headed westward through the rocky terrain. Shores and Allison were now satisfied that they were on the right trail, and when they returned to Grand Junction, they contacted Denver & Rio Grande officials.

The search was resumed the following morning, but the rocky ground made tracking slow and difficult. The men were forced to leave their horses in the canyon. The area was composed of red sandstone, and the outlaws left only occasional scratches or scuff marks on the reddish-colored rocks. A tobacco plug was found on a rock, along with a wooden-handled pocket knife with the small blade open. Apparently the robbers had cut themselves some quids and forgot the plug and knife. The blades on the knife had been filed square, allowing it to double as a screwdriver for dismantling and cleaning guns. That particular morning, in his hurry to get started, Allison had forgotten his own tobacco and was relieved to find some.

Allison held a desk job and was not accustomed to the physical exertion required to track outlaws across open country for days on end. He fell farther and farther behind during the day. Because of the concentration required to find traces of the outlaws in the rocky country, Shores forgot about Allison until it grew dark. Then Shores realized his partner was nowhere in sight and might be lost or injured. At the risk of being detected by the outlaws, Shores shouted for Allison. There was nothing but stillness. Suddenly, Allison came scrambling into view with his small British pistol in hand, calling softly, "Where are they? Where are they?"

"Where are who?" Shores asked.

"The train robbers! Didn't you hear them yelling?" was Allison's breathless reply.

Shores exclaimed, "That was me yelling for you. I thought you were lost."

Allison sat down to catch his breath. Shores reasoned that if the train robbers had traveled this far on foot out Bangs Canyon they wouldn't stop until they reached the Dolores River.

Darkness overtook the men before they could return to their horses. There was no moon that night, and the men could hardly find their way through the rocks. Shores lost his footing and tumbled down the side of the canyon into a waterhole. He landed on his holstered Colt revolver and bruised his hip. The fall also bent the stock on his Winchester rifle. The two men continued, moving cautiously over the rocks, stopping to listen for their horses. Finally they found them. They headed down the canyon, trusting the ability of their animals to find the way. It was only an hour or so before daylight when they returned to their Grand Junction hotel.

The next day Shores and Allison caught the train for Gunnison. Arrangements were made to have three good saddle horses sent by rail to a point near the mouth of Unaweep Canyon. Shores and Allison teamed up with James Duckworth, special agent for the Denver & Rio Grande Express Company. The men rode up the road through Unaweep Canyon, reasoning that the outlaws had made it across the high country to the Dolores River. It took eleven hours of riding to reach the river. That night, they stayed at a cow camp run by Tom Denning. The next morning, the men got ready to head out. Things were kind of slow for Denning, so he joined the posse. Besides, he knew the country and was welcomed as a guide.

Not far away, along the Dolores River, the posse ran across some placer miners washing gold out of the stream. One of them told Shores he had seen fresh tracks of men on foot about twelve miles to the southwest in Sinbad Valley near the Utah line. The miner remembered the tracks because it was very unusual to find human footprints in such a remote area.

Shores, Allison, Duckworth, and Denning crossed the Dolores River and headed southwest on a trail made by the Ute Indians. It was just about dark when the old Indian trail began a precipitous descent into Sinbad Valley through a forest of piñon pine and cedar trees. A number of times the horses slipped and fell on the steep, rocky trail. To add to the posse's discomfort, it began to rain.

It was nearly midnight before the men rode out into an open valley. By this time all of them were soaked to the skin. At the risk of being detected by the outlaws, several shots were fired into the air in hope that some rancher would respond and give them shelter. No response came through the stillness, only the sound of the rain. The men removed the saddles, hobbled their horses, and sat together with a blanket over their heads. They were unable to find any dry wood to build a fire to relieve their discomfort, and they were forced to sit through the cold, miserable night without one.

When dawn came, they noticed some type of primitive dwelling, practically hidden by brush, at the mouth of a small gulch. It was getting colder and still raining, making any type of shelter look good. As they approached, they realized it was a dugout set back into the bank. Logs and dirt formed its roof. Upright posts buried in the ground formed the front wall, and the makeshift door was unlocked. As they entered, it was obvious that the occupant had not been gone long. Possibly the gunshots had frightened him off. A distillery inside revealed the occupation of the owner, and moonshine whiskey was still dripping from one of the pipes. A five-gallon oil can sat nearby, two-thirds full with bootleg liquor. Naturally the posse took a sample to warm themselves, but they found the moonshine to be of rather poor quality.

The dugout was stocked with supplies. The men used some dry wood to build a warm fire in an old, rusty cookstove that sat in one corner. There was plenty of flour, lard, and coffee. Allison and Duckworth unsaddled and hobbled the horses, while Doc Shores fixed up some coffee and biscuits and fried some venison they had with them. The breakfast was washed down with more moonshine, and the spirits of the men were lifted.

The cold rain soon turned to wet snow, and the storm continued for three days. The posse remained comfortable, living on venison, moonshine, and the bootlegger's provisions. The men expected the occupant to return any time, but possibly out of fear of being arrested, he never did.

The storm broke on the fourth day, and the sun came out on the white landscape. The tracks of the fugitives were obliterated by the snow. Before leaving the dugout, Doc Shores left a note for the occupant that concluded: "We invite you to come and call on us if you ever come over into our respective parts of the country, and we'll try to return the compliment." It was signed by Doc Shores, M. L. Allison, and Jim Duckworth. The remaining portion of the deer was left behind as compensation for the use of the dugout.

Shores guessed that the outlaws originally planned to hide in Sinbad Valley until it was safe to leave. He also guessed that the snowstorm had forced them to seek lower elevations. For this reason, the posse rode south to Paradox Valley, hoping to pick up the trail. After making inquiries of the hired hands at a ranch and determining that no one had seen any tracks, the posse returned to Grand Junction. The heavy snow, however, forced the men to detour down the Dolores River to the present site of Bedrock, then follow the San Miguel River to the present site of Uravan. Here the men stayed two nights at a ranch to wait out another snowstorm. After the weather improved, they rode to Placerville.

The cold and exposure had taken their toll, however, and Jim Duckworth became ill on the way back. The other men did everything they could to lessen his burden during the trip, but Duckworth grew worse. At Placerville, Duckworth and Shores took the stage to Dallas. From there, Duckworth returned to Denver by train to recuperate. He came down with pneumonia, however, and died a few days later. It was a high price to pay for chasing outlaws.

Shores met Allison and Denning at Montrose and traveled on to Delta. Here they learned some interesting information. Shortly before the train robbery, four strangers had come into Delta on foot, leading a packhorse. They set up camp near town and spent several days constructing a boat. Several townspeople stopped to watch them as boat building was a very unusual activity in Delta. The strangers said they had traveled over the mountains from Carbondale, where they were employed on the Colorado Midland Railroad. Delta residents learned that two of the men were brothers by the names of Jack and Bob Smith. They were big men and had dark hair. Their companions were Ed Rhodes, a medium-sized man with blond hair, and Bob Wallace, a small, wiry individual with red hair and a red mustache. Only circumstantial evidence linked them with the holdup at Unaweep Switch. They did have guns and supplies, which they loaded into the boat a short time before the train robbery. The Pinkerton Detective Agency was contacted to find out what it could about these men.

After a false lead involving a trip up the Colorado River to Ravens Beak, Tom Denning became very ill and ran a high fever. He was unable to ride and had to be taken to Grand Junction by wagon. Unlike Duckworth, Denning later recovered. Shores was sent on a second wild goose chase to Kansas. Despite the excellent lead they discovered in Delta, the manhunt seemed to be falling apart.

Next, Doc Shores was called to Denver by the Pinkerton Detective Agency to receive new information about the case. At the same time, a report came in that four men had come down the Colorado River in a boat and had gone through Cisco,

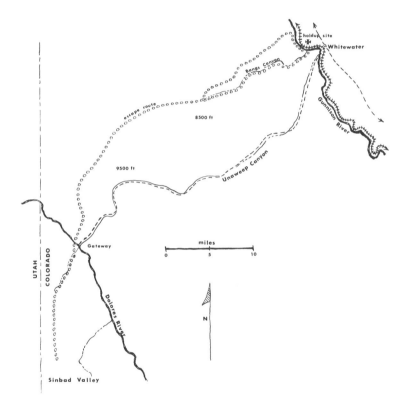

Utah, west of Grand Junction. The men had then caught a freight train headed north toward Salt Lake City. Shores had no choice but to send his undersheriff and Allison on to Utah while he went to Denver.

Allison and the undersheriff learned that the men they were after were in the Price River area. It was here that three of the train robbers were arrested: Ed Rhodes, Jack Smith, and Bob Smith. The fourth outlaw, Bob Wallace, was no longer with them. Shores was probably disappointed that he was not on hand to savor the victory and enjoy the capture of the train robbers after having spent so much time and energy in the chase. For him, the end seemed anticlimactic.

When Shores received the news of the capture, he caught the next train west and managed to intercept his undersheriff and Allison, with their three prisoners, on an eastbound Denver & Rio Grande train at Thompson's Springs, Utah.

Now Doc Shores was able to meet face to face the men he had tracked for so many miles. He introduced himself and began the conversation, "Well, you fellows have sure been causin' me a lot of grief, trackin' you all over the country."

Ed Rhodes spoke up, "You're the damndest bloodhound I ever seen, but the last couple of months ain't been no harder on you than on us. We've been living outdoors in this damned weather, freezin' and starvin' like wild animals."

Jack Smith quickly added, "That's right. In a way I'm glad you finally caught up with us. I ain't been warm or had a square meal since the robbery."

Shores noticed that Jack's face was bandaged. He asked about it.

Smith said, "Ed here accidentally shot me with his shotgun while we were hiding out in Bangs Canyon."

"He was hurt so bad," continued Bob Smith, "that I walked clear back to the river intending to go into Grand Junction to get a doctor. But when I seen the big posse down in the valley looking for us, I lost my nerve and turned back. I expected to find Jack dead, but when I got back he was sitting up, smoking a cigarette!"

The outlaws and lawmen continued to compare notes like old buddies rather than adversaries. Among other things, Shores learned that Bob Wallace's real name was Bob Boyle. With three of the four outlaws in a Denver jail pending trial before a federal court, Shores went about hunting down the last man. He visited Boyle's family in Paola, Kansas. It was a long, complicated journey, but he learned that Bob Boyle was working on an irrigation canal near Price, Utah. Lacking a warrant or extradition papers, Shores hunted the last train robber carefully. Boyle was whisked out of Utah and turned over to authorities in Gunnison. Shores was paid three thousand dollars by the Denver & Rio Grande Express Company and one thousand dollars by the federal government. It is assumed that he split some of his reward money with Denning and Allison.

About twenty years later, Doc Shores met Jack Smith on Grand Junction's main street. The meeting was accidental, but despite the long lapse in time, the two men recognized each other. The scar from the shotgun wound received in Bangs Canyon was noticeable on Smith's face. Shores learned that Jack had settled down in Whitewater, just a mile or so from Unaweep Switch. Bob Smith and Bob Boyle were somewhere in Alaska and had stayed on the right side of the law. Ed Rhodes had been shot to death in an argument while working near Boulder.

References

"Rio Grande Robbers." *Rocky Mountain News*, November 4, 1887, p. 1, cols. 1, 2.

Rockwell, Wilson. *Memoirs of a Lawman*. Denver: Sage Books, 1962, pp. 145-183.

Shores, C. W. "The First Train Robbery on the Denver & Rio Grande in 1887." Manuscript, January 10, 1928. Western History Department, Denver Public Library.

———. "Train Robberies—Express Robberies on Rio Grande Railroad." Manuscript, April 19, 1929. Western History Department, Denver Public Library.

Jack Wight and George Witherill killed S. K. Wall, a sheepherder, in Douglas County, south of Denver, on September 17, 1871. The purpose of the murder was to rob Wall of his money and his sheep. *From Cook, Hands Up!, 1897 ed.*

George Witherill Lynched in Canon City

O ne of the minor tributaries of the South Platte River flowing north from Douglas County is Dry Creek. It is a stream that flows mainly during spring runoff or in periods of wet weather. The creekbed in Douglas County is skirted with underbrush, willows, and a few cottonwoods. Dry Creek runs for twenty miles or so through a region that was primarily used for grazing sheep. During the early history of Colorado, this part of Douglas County was populated by a few ranchers and sheepherders.

S. K. Wall moved into the Dry Creek area during the late 1860s. He lived the quiet, lonely life of a sheepherder and, on occasion, rode into Denver to take care of his banking and to purchase supplies. He would also buy books to fill his life of solitude. Wall lived in a dugout he had built from a fallen willow tree, along the bank of Dry Creek. His frugal hermit's life led to speculation among the residents of the area that he had a great deal of money stashed in his dugout.

One of Wall's neighbors was a Mr. LeFevre, who employed a young man named George H. Witherill as a sheepherder. Another neighbor, J. S. McCool, had an employee named E. E. "Jack" Wight. Both Witherill and Wight were in their twenties. Not much else was known about either man other than that Jack Wight was from Iowa, and George Witherill was a native of New York state.

Witherill and Wight were soon good friends and began work on a plot to appropriate Wall's property, including his four hundred sheep. Although they were both sheepherders and worked miles apart for different owners, they managed to set up meetings to do their planning. They reasoned that the only logical way to steal Wall's property was simply to kill him. These plans began to take root during the summer of 1871.

On Sunday, September 17, the two men took the day off to put their plan into action. They met in the early afternoon, at around three o'clock. Witherill was on horseback, and Wight was on foot. Witherill gave Wight his gun as they approached Wall, who was relaxing on a hillside, watching his sheep. After striking up a casual conversation, Wight drew his gun and fired at Wall. The sheepherder fell, but much to the men's surprise, he got back on his feet and began running down the hillside toward Dry Creek. Wight took off after Wall, shooting whenever he could, while Witherill followed on his horse. Wall soon became faint from loss of blood from the wound in his chest and was forced to sit down in the creekbed. Witherill dismounted and joined his partner as they walked over to Wall.

"What does this mean?" Wall said.

One of the men replied, "Mean? It means that you are having too good a time of it—that you are making too much money and a damn old snoozer who knows no better how to use it and enjoy it than you do. We want it. We want your sheep, your money, everything you've got, damn you!"

The poor fellow was now rapidly sinking from loss of blood and could only reply, "Take everything, but spare my life. I don't want to die. I have done nothing to deserve death. I will give you everything freely. All I ask is that I be permitted to live." [1] The poor fellow continued to plead for his life. The heavy barrel of a rifle was brought down on Wall's skull while the other man fired point blank into Wall.

Witherill and Wight believed that Wall had lots of gold and silver stored in his dugout. But first they searched Wall's pockets, taking a watch and twelve dollars. They also found a certificate of deposit for three hundred dollars at a Denver bank. The body was buried quickly under a pile of rocks next to the creek bank, almost at the point where Wall had fallen.

The murderers then walked to Wall's dugout a short distance away. They began their search, but contrary to their expectations, they found nothing of any value.

The following morning, Witherill rode into Denver. He went to the office of a lawyer and, pretending he was Wall, had a bill of sale for the sheep made out to himself. He forged Wall's name on it so that later he could demonstrate he had legal title to the sheep. The following day, Witherill rounded up Wall's sheep. A few days later, he rode back to Denver and put an ad in the *Rocky Mountain News* for their sale.

Local residents noticed Witherill in charge of Wall's sheep, and they also noticed Wall's absence. When questioned, George Witherill produced the forged bill of sale and told his neighbors that Wall had sold out and left the state.

What seemed suspicious was that George Witherill never had a dime to his name and couldn't have raised enough money as a sheepherder to buy Wall out. Also, George was wearing Wall's watch. Some of the residents of the Dry Creek area rode into Denver and presented these facts to the Rocky Mountain Detective Agency, headed by General David J. Cook. Cook also happened to be sheriff of Arapahoe County. These facts, in turn, were presented by Cook to the sheriff of Douglas County.

Witherill's next move was to ride to Denver to try to cash the certificate of deposit. The clerk at the bank reported that the endorsement was not in Wall's handwriting. Witherill was flustered and maintained that Wall was in Laramie. He told the clerk he would get it endorsed again. After Witherill left, the clerk contacted local authorities. About two weeks later, Witherill showed up again at the bank and tried a second time to cash the certificate. This time the endorsement was in a different handwriting. Again the clerk refused to cash it, and under instructions from the Rocky Mountain Detective Agency, kept the certificate.

Witherill and Wight were extremely disappointed in how little money their brutal crime had yielded. They rustled about six hundred sheep from J. K. Doolittle and merged them with Wall's sheep. The theft was soon reported, and George Hopkins, Denver's city marshal, was dispatched to recover the stolen sheep and to arrest George Witherill. The sheep were easy to find. When the marshal approached Witherill, he showed him the forged bill of sale for Wall's sheep. Witherill was taken into custody and brought to Denver, where he was identified as the man who had forged Wall's name on the bill of sale. He was also identified as the man who had tried to cash the certificate of deposit.

Before David Cook found out about this, Witherill had been released and was on his way back to Douglas County. Cook decided to have him arrested a second time and hold him in jail until a thorough investigation could be completed into the disappearance of S. K. Wall.

So far, Jack Wight had remained above suspicion and had cleverly kept out of sight while letting Witherill do all the dirty work. A day after Witherill left Denver, Wight went to the authorities and advised them to arrest Witherill. He told them he believed that George Witherill had killed Wall. This bold and devious move was designed to lift any suspicion that he was connected to Witherill. He knew, however, that if Witherill were arrested a second time and questioned, he would talk. As part of his plan, Wight rode hard for the Dry Creek area and warned Witherill that the law was after him for murder. It was easy to talk Witherill into leaving, but the odd part of the story is that Wight went with him. Wight may have felt he would ultimately be implicated in the crime.

On October 12, 1871, almost a month after Wall's murder, David Cook dispatched two of his best men to arrest George Witherill. When they arrived in the Dry Creek area, they quickly learned that both Wight and Witherill had disappeared. They also discovered that several valuable horses were missing from area ranches.

The detectives began to search the area in the vicinity of Wall's dugout for clues. As they were walking up the creekbed, they noticed some wolves standing around a pile of stones along the bank. The animals were pawing and sniffing the pile of rocks. The detectives fired at the wolves to drive them off. As they walked up to the rock pile, they saw the fleshless arm of a human being. The stones were quickly rolled away to reveal the badly decomposed body of S. K. Wall. It was now clear that Witherill and possibly Wight were involved in the murder.

In the meantime, Jack Wight and George Witherill were enduring the hardships of the vast prairie. They avoided all roads, ranches, and towns, resting during the day and riding at night. By the fifth day, they were exhausted and out of food. They spotted a large herd of buffalo. As they rode into the herd, they singled out an old bull and fired at him, wounding him so badly he couldn't keep up with the rest of the herd. They rode up alongside the animal to issue the final volley. Just as Wight was about to fire his rifle at point blank range into the bull's neck, Witherill came riding up from behind and fired his pistol into the back of the animal. The shot so startled the bull that he

While attempting to escape from the law, Witherill and Wight hunted down an old buffalo bull. As Wight got close to the wounded animal, it turned on him and ripped his leg open with its horn. *From Cook Hands Up!, 1897 ed.*

lunged at Wight's horse. The bison's horn caught Wight in the shin and ripped open a wound from the calf all the way to the knee. Wight spurred his horse to escape another lunge. Both men rode off, leaving the wounded animal behind.

Wight's leg was bound and at the next ranch they introduced themselves as buffalo hunters. They asked if they could stay for a while until Wight could recover sufficiently to continue the ride. After two days, gangrene set in, and the two men decided to take their chances to seek medical help. At Julesburg, George Witherill helped Wight onto a train bound for North Platte, Nebraska. It was Witherill's intention to follow on horseback.

Back in Denver, Dave Cook had a good idea that the fugitives had fled east. Descriptions were sent out, and it wasn't too long before a deputy sheriff telegraphed Cook that he had captured Witherill. The deputy had learned that two strangers had entered Julesburg, so he began to search the town after dark. He found Witherill asleep in a barn with his guns lying around him. He was arrested but maintained his name was William Jackson. Later he confessed and even told the officers that Jack Wight was on a train headed to North Platte, Nebraska. Once Witherill had been turned over to David Cook, the deputy sheriff was given one hundred dollars to hunt down Wight. The following morning, the lawman returned with Wight, and both fugitives were taken to the Arapahoe County jail in Denver.

Originally, the trial was to take place in Frankstown, the county seat in Douglas County. A change of venue was obtained to move the trial to Evans. Both men escaped the gallows because of loopholes in Colorado law. Wight's complicity in Wall's murder was difficult to prove except through Witherill's testimony. Wight was set free on a two thousand dollar bond on the charge of horse theft, although he was later found guilty. Witherill, on the other hand, made a full confession and was sentenced to life in the state penitentiary in Canon City.

For several months, Wight served his sentence for horse theft in the Arapahoe County jail in Denver, but Witherill was sent south to begin his stay in the penitentiary. While in jail, Wight made a desperate effort to escape, and as a result was sentenced to seven years of hard labor, also at the state penitentiary. After two years, Wight escaped. He was captured four years later in Maine and returned to Canon City to serve out his term.

In 1887, Colorado passed a law defining a life sentence as only sixteen years of incarceration. As a result, George R. Witherill was released on April 18, 1887. Due in part to the subsequent events, the Colorado legislature later repealed this limited-sentence law.

Because General David Cook had blocked Witherill's pardon several times, the murderer headed immediately to Denver to kill the famous detective. When he met Cook, however, Witherill just threw up his hands. Cook gave him some strong advice, including the suggestion to leave Denver and never return.

George Witherill did leave Denver: he became a miner, drifted to Durango, then went to Ironton near Red Mountain Pass. While living in Ironton, he made friends with a Swede named Marinus Jansen. The Swede owned a splendid, four-horse team and a big ore wagon. He did a lively business with the mines in the area. Under the pretense of having part ownership in a Silverton mine, Witherill convinced Jansen to go with him over the mountain with Jansen's team and wagon to pick up a load of rich ore. The two men left in early September 1887, and that was the last that was seen of Jansen. Toward the end of the month, Witherill drove the ore wagon to Pueblo and sold the outfit for four hundred dollars.

Next, Witherill hired Charles R. McCain to haul ore in the Canon City area. He promised McCain a lucrative job using McCain's two teams and wagons. Witherill represented himself as the foreman of a big mine. The two men, each handling one of the wagons, left Pueblo the morning of October 25.

When night came, they stopped at Beaver Creek, some eighteen miles from their destination. Both men lay down in the beds of their wagons. Witherill waited until McCain was asleep, then crept over to his wagon. At point-blank range, he fired his rifle into McCain's head. The bullet passed through the man's brain, out the bed of the wagon and flattened itself on a rock. As if this weren't enough, Witherill sadistically took an ax and pounded McCain's head into a mass of broken bone and brain matter.

Witherill then dragged McCain's lifeless body into a ravine, where he covered it with rocks and dirt. To destroy evidence of the bloodstains, he set fire to some hay in the bed of the wagon, then rubbed the wood with a stone.

As if nothing had happened, Witherill took both wagons and their teams into Canon City the next morning. While in town, he wrote McCain's wife, whom he had met before leaving Pueblo with McCain, pretending to be her husband. He informed her that he had purchased a ranch near Grand Junction and had sold the teams. He then asked her to sell all her household goods and join him as soon as possible. It is not known what devious plan Witherill had in mind next.

When Mrs. McCain received the letter she knew immediately it was a forgery. She instinctively felt something was dreadfully wrong. She contacted a local law officer and notices were sent out alerting people to watch for George Witherill. Deputy Sheriff Force was sent out from Denver to find Witherill. He met his man on the road from Canon City, but the murderer claimed his name was Simon Cotter. Force responded, "That may be your name now, but it wasn't Simon Cotter or Simon Says Thumbs Up when I saw you in the pen at Canon [City]." The ex-convict submitted to arrest in silence.

When the wagon was examined closely, the bloodstains were found. The ax was also found, with blood on its handle. McCain's wallet was discovered on Witherill, along with $250 in cash. Witherill told officials he had left McCain alive and well in Canon City, but the evidence against him grew when McCain's body was found on November 1.

On the afternoon of November 2, Witherill was taken by a local sheriff toward Canon City. Reports reached the sheriff that a lynch mob was waiting anxiously for Witherill's return. The sheriff deviated from his plan and stopped in Pueblo, where Witherill was locked up for a few days. The prisoner was then returned to the Arapahoe County jail in Denver. Law officers waited a month until they believed things had cooled down in Canon City. On December 3, Witherill was placed in the baggage car of a Denver & Rio Grande train. Five miles from Canon City, he was transferred, under heavy guard, to a carriage. He was then transported the rest of the way to town and locked up. All those involved tried to keep his trip a secret, but somehow the residents of Canon City knew George Witherill was back in town.

Early in the evening, small crowds began to gather on the street corners. Sheriff Griffth tried to calm the crowd, but it was useless. Later in the evening, a small band of Canon City's young men, somewhat under the influence, went to the jail. The men were loud and obnoxious. They stood around the jail and threatened to harm the sheriff if he didn't release Witherill to them to be hung. The sheriff's pregnant wife was so frightened, a doctor was called, for fear she would lose her baby. When the mob finally realized that Sheriff Griffth was not going to give up his prisoner, it dispersed.

Meanwhile, on the other side of town, a quiet group of citizens carefully put together a plan to lynch George Witherill. There were no drunks among these men. As soon as the young men had left the jail, a lookout notified them. It was about 3:30 A.M. when they quietly surrounded the jail and stood in position.

The sheriff heard a soft rap on the west door of the jail. Someone quietly spoke his name, and he asked what was wanted. The voice told him a friend was waiting outside with some important information. The sheriff drew his revolver and handed the jail keys to his sixteen-year-old son. Slowly, the sheriff turned the latch on the door, but as soon as he opened it, a dozen men burst into the jail, throwing him to the floor. He yelled for help but was quickly bound and gagged. The men dragged the struggling sheriff to a guard house about a hundred yards from the jail.

The son tried to help his father, but the odds against him were too great. In the scuffle, the keys to the jail were found. The mob rushed to Witherill's cell, and as the prisoner heard the men approach, he broke off a leg from his bed. He was ready to fight. A few of the men entered the cell, and Witherill struck out at them, smashing the lamp. When a match was lit, the prisoner struck again but missed. Immediately, two shots were fired in the darkness into the cell. Both missed. There was a moment of silence, then a noise came from the cell. A third shot was fired, shattering Witherill's shoulder blade. The wounded man was forced to give in. His hands were tied behind his back.

The murderer was dragged out of his cell, out into the dark street, and pushed to the nearest telegraph pole. A member of the mob quickly climbed the pole and threw a line over one of the crossarms. A noose was tied and placed around Witherill's neck, and the condemned man was given a minute to confess to the murders of Wall, Jansen, and McClain. He refused and was hoisted into the air until his feet were five or six feet from the

Early in the morning on December 4, 1888, an angry Canon City lynch mob pulled George Witherill from his cell and hung him from a telegraph pole for the murder of three men. *Colorado Historical Society*

ground. Just at the point of suffocation, he was lowered and given a second chance to confess. Again he refused by shaking his head. This time he was drawn halfway up the pole, and the rope was tied off. The crowd watched his agonizing death with little sign of remorse.

When daylight came, George Witherill's lifeless body swayed in the gentle breeze. Many residents came out to view his remains, which hung in plain view of the state penitentiary where he had spent sixteen years. At nine o'clock, the county coroner cut the body down. An inquest was held immediately, with the following verdict: "The said jurors, upon their oath, do swear that said George R. Witherill came to his death on the morn of December 4, A. D. 1888, by being hung by the neck by persons or person to the jury unknown."

Notes

1. The account of this conversation is recorded in *Hands Up!* by John W. Cook. It may have been taken from a confession made by George Witherill to General David Cook after his capture.

References

Collier, William Ross and Edwin Victor Westrate. *Dave Cook of the Rockies.* New York: Rufus Rockwell Wilson, 1936, pp. 116–121.

Cook, John W. *Hands Up! or Thirty-Five Years of Detective Life in the Mountains and on the Plains.* Denver: W. F. Robinson Printing Co., 1897, pp. 177–212.

Mangan, Terry William. *Colorado on Glass.* Denver: Sundance Limited, 1975, p. 270

"A Murderer Strung Up." *Rocky Mountain News,* December 5, 1888, p. 1, col. 1.

Cyrus Wells "Doc" Shores quelled the 1891 coal miners strike in Crested Butte. At the time, Shores was Gunnison's sheriff and a highly respected lawman. *Western History Department, Denver Public Library*

Miners Strike at Crested Butte

G unnison's famous sheriff, Cyrus Wells "Doc" Shores, received a telegram dated December 11, 1891, from the superintendent of the Colorado Coal & Iron Co. at Crested Butte. The telegram stated that striking coal miners had stopped the fans to their coal mine. The superintendent urged Doc Shores to help out, since an explosion was imminent unless the fans were restarted to clear the mine of dangerous coal gas.

The strike had been precipitated by the reduction in wages for the miners from seventy-five cents/ton to sixty-five cents/ton. The CC&I claimed that increased competition from Utah mines had forced it to reduce its selling price on coke by fifty cents/ton. Additional pressure came from the Denver & Rio Grande Railroad to lower the price on locomotive coal by twenty-five cents/ton.

The mine was located on the south side of Crested Butte and was one of several in the area. The five hundred workers were predominantly Austrian and Italian immigrants. Most of them had left their families behind, and they lived in cramped boarding houses. The miners planned to return to their homelands, rich from their stay in the United States. At the time of the strike, Crested Butte had a population of around fifteen hundred.

Drinking was about the only amusement after hours. The miners worked from seven in the morning to six at night every day except Sunday. When they got off work, the bars were packed with singing, drunken men. Shores liked these hard-working, hard-drinking miners and prized their friendship. He was disappointed over the lawlessness that erupted during the strike.

Around the first of December, when the strike first began, Shores went to Crested Butte to talk to the miners. He told them that they had every right to go on strike, but that they didn't have the right to endanger life or to destroy property. He warned them he would return if there were any trouble.

While traveling back to Gunnison by train, Doc Shores met the roadmaster for the Denver & Rio Grande. He told Shores that the situation was tense in Crested Butte, and that if he returned, the strikers planned to cut off his head and carry it through the streets of town.

As soon as Doc Shores got back to Gunnison, he organized a posse of twenty-four men. The railroad provided a special train for the trip to Crested Butte, consisting of two coaches plus the locomotive. The members of the posse were deputized and placed on one of the coaches; the other coach contained mine officials and a Catholic priest. Shores left strict instructions for the telegraph operator in Gunnison not to wire Crested Butte about the special train.

It was getting quite late and the engineer ran the twenty-eight miles up to Crested Butte as fast as he could. It was around midnight when the special train pulled up to the depot. To prevent detection, the headlight on the locomotive was switched off. The engineer did not blow the whistle for the crossings as he approached town. With two feet of snow on the ground and temperature well below zero, the evening was still.

The car with the mine officials and the Catholic priest was uncoupled and left at the depot. Some switching was done, and the car with the posse was pushed ahead of the locomotive toward the mine entrance. The train moved past a long pile of coking coal about ten feet high. Suddenly, a group of men came running toward the train, shooting as they approached. The miners knew about the special train. The Gunnison telegraph operator was a strong union man and had wired the Crested Butte operator to spread the word. This allowed the Italian workers to arm themselves and to organize an ambush.

The engineer set the brakes, uncoupled the car, and returned to the depot, leaving the car stranded. Doc Shores and his posse crouched below the windows as bullets shattered the glass.

The mayor of Crested Butte, John Tetard, reached the door to the coach ahead of the mob. "You're sittin' ducks in here, Doc," he cried above the shots. "Get your men out of the car as quick as you can."

The striking miners were only a couple of hundred yards

In December 1891, there was a strike by the coal miners at Crested Butte. Gunnison Sheriff Doc Shores was called in to restore law and order. A confrontation between law officers and miners occurred in which thirty-six strikers were wounded. *Colorado Historical Society, photograph by George L. Bean*

away. Bullets ricocheted off the coach body as Doc Shores moved his men to the opposite side of the coach.

"I think we can make it to the coal chute. Let's run for it," yelled Mayor Tetard.

The coal chute was about 200 yards from the coach. A shed led from the chute to the mine entrance to protect the tracks from heavy winter snows. A stairway led up to the chute, and Doc Shores figured that if they could make it, they could hold off an army. As the possee began its dash for the stairway, the miners began firing all types of weapons, including shotguns, rifles, and pistols. Fortunately, the shots went wide or whistled overhead. But as the posse dashed past the long pile of coke, Doc knew they would be overtaken before they could reach safety.

He yelled to his men, "Get down behind the tracks. We've got to make our stand here." The raised grade of the railroad formed a bulwark. Shores directed his men not to fire until he gave the command. It was about one o'clock in the morning, and the men were forced to lie stretched out in the snow in sub-zero temperatures. Outnumbered nearly five to one, the posse waited with its rifles pointed at the approaching mob. Doc continued to direct his men, "Remember to aim low when you shoot since we don't want to kill anybody if we can help it."

Under the hypnotic influence of mob hysteria, the strikers yelled out in their native tongue. Some insults were hurled at the posse in English. The mob taunted Shores to come out in the open and fight like a man. Another striker said that they were going to work him over.

Three of the deputies cracked under the pressure and jumped to their feet. Two ran off into the night, the other one crashed into a coal car standing on a siding. The remaining men asked when they could shoot. Shores told them to stay low where they couldn't get hit. The men held their Winchesters cocked and ready. The strikers were bunched up, and when they were about twenty-five yards away, Shores yelled, "All right, give 'em hell."

The Winchesters barked almost at the same time and the volley caused more than two dozen strikers to fall to the ground. Many were not hit initially but simply fell over their comrades. The posse continued to pour deadly fire into the crowd. Most of the miners panicked and fled back to town. Some shot back as they ran. A few hid behind trees and exchanged shots with the posse. One of the deputies got so excited that he pumped fourteen cartridges out of the magazine of his rifle without firing a shot. In all, the *Rocky Mountain News* reported that more than two hundred rounds were fired.

The shooting finally died down, and Shores directed his men to run for the stairway leading to the coal chute. They made it to safety. As they looked down into the town of Crested Butte, they could see women and children coming up to help the wounded men back to town. Many of the wounded lay motionless on the bloodstained snow. In all, thirty-six strikers had been hit. Of those, only one man was seriously wounded. He was a portly Italian who was shooting at the posse from behind a small tree, using a new Marlin rifle he had borrowed. The tree had failed to protect him, and he was hit three times in the back. He later recovered from his wounds. The only wounded posse member was the fellow who ran into the parked coal car.

The men in the posse now realized they were stuck for the night at an elevation of nine thousand feet with no food or blankets. They didn't dare build a fire for fear it might attract a sharpshooter. None of the men wanted to risk going into town, since it appeared there was a lot of activity on the streets.

After an uncomfortable night, they watched the town come to life at dawn. They still didn't dare send a group to the depot to wire for supplies.

Late in the morning, several miners walked out of the Elk Mountain Hotel where, evidently, a meeting had been held. These miners began to walk up toward the coal chute, and as they walked, they showed that they were unarmed. They walked up to the bottom of the stairway and asked where Mayor Tetard was. The mayor answered and stepped forward into view.

One of the miners announced, "We have been appointed as a committee to inform you that the citizens and miners of Crested Butte have just passed a resolution asking you to resign."

The mayor's reply was brisk. "You can go back and tell your cohorts that maybe they can beat me at the next election, but there will be no resignation."

"You'd better think it over," threatened the miner. "Everyone is pretty mad at the way you deserted us last night and went over to the enemy."

Mayor Tetard reminded them that Doc Shores and his men were not their enemies and that they came to Crested Butte only to protect private property. Tetard concluded, "They're just trying to do their duty, the same as I am."

The miner spoke, "Maybe you call it that, but we don't. Tell Shores to take his men and go back to Gunnison."

Another miner called out, "Sheriff, the miners and citizens of Crested Butte demand that you and your men get out of town."

Shores knew many of the miners and happened to recognize the speaker. He spoke to him directly, "Mike, when I was up here several days ago, I told you fellows that you have a perfect right to go on strike so long as you didn't violate the law and endanger life or property. By refusing to let the engineers keep the fans going, you did both, and that's why I'm here."

Mike then asked, "Why didn't you come in the daytime like a man instead of sneaking up here at night?"

"My term as sheriff has nearly expired, but I want to make it clear once and for all that so long as I'm sheriff of this county I will go any place I please at any time I please." This put an end to the exchange of words, and the miners returned to the town knowing that Doc Shores was going to continue to hold the mine.

Several posse members descended from the coal chute to retrieve some of the guns that were scattered about on the snow. The Marlin rifle used by the most seriously wounded man was brought back. Later in the afternoon, two Italians walked up from town to the base of the stairs and asked for Doc Shores. They asked if a new Marlin rifle had been found, and Doc responding by holding up the gun, asking, "Is this it?"

The response was, "Yes, that's my rifle. I loaned it last night to one of my friends, and he got shot up and lost it. Can I have it back?"

"No, I'm keeping it as state's evidence. In the future," advised Shores, "be more careful who you lend guns to." The two miners walked back toward town gesturing to each other in an animated manner.

Members of the posse were very reluctant to spend a second freezing night without food or blankets at the mine. One man volunteered to sneak down to Gunnison to get some supplies.

Shores advised waiting a little longer, but it was around four o'clock, and the shadows were now reaching across the valley.

In the distance, the men noticed a horse-drawn sleigh coming down Main Street. On it were piled blankets and supplies. The posse could also see guns poking out of some of the windows and doors as the sleigh passed slowly through town. Fortunately, no one stopped it, and the sleigh pulled up to the mine. The two men on the sleigh were from Gunnison, and the supplies were a gift from the people of the town. The mine officials in the second railroad car had observed the shooting the night before, and they promptly returned to Gunnison. The officials had believed that in the heavy exchange of gunfire the posse members were either killed or wounded. The alarm spread through Gunnison, and the townspeople put together what they could.

After the supplies and blankets had been distributed, the morale of the men was restored. An hour later, a special train pulled up to the mine loaded with thirty-five new deputies and several mine officials. Shores released ten of the original posse members so they could return home and recover from exposure.

In the meantime, the mine continued to fill with explosive coal gas. Shores threatened to take his men home if the mine officials didn't get the fans going to clear the mine. Soon they got the engine started, and the fans began to hum.

The miners now issued a list of their demands and complaints:

1. The wage was to be returned from its present rate of sixty-five cents/ton to seventy-five cents/ton and remain no lower than that forever.

2. The miners said they were forced to carry the mine supports too far and that this reduced productivity. They wanted more supports closer to their work.

3. They also complained that they had to push the empty mine cars too far before loading. The miners demanded that more cars be added to alleviate this problem.

Miners were making from $56/month up to $108/month. Cokemen earned from $58/month to $79/month, and common laborers received $57/month.

After a cooling-off period of a few days, four deputies and Doc Shores went into town for a meeting at the Elk Mountain Hotel with mine officials and representatives from the striking miners. Shores selected his best gunmen, including Jack Watson, a former Texas ranger; and the Marlow brothers, who were still wanted in Texas but whom Governor Routt refused to extradite because of extenuating circumstances.[1] The deputies had been warned that virtually every man in Crested Butte was armed. Each of Doc Shores's men wore two six-shooters under his overcoat, and they each carried a Winchester rifle. From the coal chute, the remaining deputies kept an eye on the hotel in case of trouble.

The outcome of the meeting was that the company wanted to reduce its labor force from 250 to 200, but to keep the sixty-five cents/ton rate. The reduction in labor would allow the remaining men to mine more coal per day. The idea was to give the men a chance to keep their overall wages the same by working harder. The company agreed to correct the other grievances.

After a couple of days, the Austrians agreed to go back to work under the company's terms. The Italians, on the other hand, continued to hold out. On December 18, Shores and a group of his best deputies began arresting the ringleaders for conspiracy. The first stop was the depot where Italian strikers were posted to look for scab labor brought in to break the strike. One swarthy man by the name of Jim Barto was arrested. After reading him the warrant, Shores took him into custody. Shores then walked down Crested Butte's main street with his deputies. They walked two abreast with each man carrying a Winchester rifle. Jim Barto, with two officers, brought up the rear. All of the saloons and businesses were located on either side of the main street, and spectators watched the procession with a great deal of interest. The law had returned to Crested Butte.

Shores and his men went into each saloon seeking out specific troublemakers. At John Follette's saloon, Shores entered with his Winchester in one hand and a warrant in the other. Follette came forward and asked in a good-natured manner, "Well, Doc, what can I serve you this morning?"

Showing little emotion, Shores answered, "This is a business call. I've come to arrest you for helping to incite the ambush on us the other night." And so it went, as Shores and his men rounded up a number of the men involved in the ambush. The ones Shores couldn't find that day were arrested later when they showed up to collect their paychecks.

Elk Avenue, Crested Butte's main street, looked like this at the time of the 1891 coal miners strike. It was down this street that Doc Shores walked with his heavily armed deputies, seeking out troublemakers. *Western History Department, Denver Public Library*

Within a few days, the mine reopened, and life in Crested Butte returned to normal.

Notes

1. George and Charley Marlow arrived in Ouray County in 1891 and took up a homestead between Ridgeway and Ouray. They became two of the finest deputies the sheriff of Ouray ever had. Doc Shores specifically requested the loan of the Marlow brothers to help quell the strike at Crested Butte. They were even brought to Gunnison by special train. Their background, however, is one of the strangest in the history of crime and justice.

In 1885, the family of Dr. William Marlow moved from Missouri to Texas. There were five boys in the family: George, Charley, Alfred, Lewellyn, and Boone. In late August 1888, two deputy U.S. marshals arrested four of the brothers on a case they were unable to crack. The marshals needed to arrest somebody in order to hold their jobs. Not a shred of evidence supported their actions.

George was the one brother not arrested, and when he tried to secure bail for his brothers, he too was jailed. Finally, their mother got her sons released. The deputies feared loss of face and began to spread vicious lies about the Marlow brothers. They managed to secure an indictment against Boone for another unsolved crime, the murder of a local resident.

Sheriff Wallace had befriended the brothers while they were in jail, but he ended up having to go with one of his deputies to arrest Boone. His deputy, Tom Collier, walked directly to the door of the Marlow cabin, while the sheriff made his way around the back. Boone greeted the deputy cordially, but Collier drew his gun and fired at Boone. The shot missed, and Boone grabbed a Winchester rifle from his bed. Collier retreated, and Boone fired through the door. As Boone ran out the door, he saw, out of the corner of his eye, another man coming around the corner of the cabin. He fired and fatally wounded his friend Sheriff Wallace. Overwhelmed by his sorrow, Boone forced Collier back into the cabin and was about to kill him when one of his brothers stepped in.

Possibly because of suspicions that all the brothers were involved in killing Sheriff Wallace, they were soon back in jail, except for Boone, who fled and was never seen in the area again. (He was later poisoned by Indians.)

On June 19, 1889, the Marlow brothers were to be transferred to a jail sixty miles away. They were chained and placed in one of three hacks. The other hacks contained the guards. The hacks had not traveled three miles before the one carrying the prisoners suddenly stopped. A mob of one hundred men opened fire on the unarmed prisoners. Charley and Alfred, although shackled, ran to the other hack and grabbed the Winchesters from the guards. George and Lewellyn overpowered another guard and secured a rifle and a pistol. In the gun battle that followed, Alfred and Lewellyn were killed, along with two or more of the vigilantes.

By cutting off the feet of their dead brothers, George and Charley freed themselves. The vigilantes tried to make it seem as if Boone had tried to rescue his brothers. In 1890 a Dallas court tried the Marlows for horse stealing, but the tide of public opinion had turned in favor of them. They were acquitted. The surviving family members successfully sued members of the vigilante group and were awarded damages. Having had their fill of Texas justice, the remaining two brothers moved to Colorado.

A pair of Texas rangers arrived in Ouray in 1891. They attempted to arrest George and Charley for their involvement in the death of Sheriff Wallace. After being informed of the facts, Governor Routt refused to sign the necessary extradition papers.

References

Brown, Robert L. *An Empire of Silver*. Caldwell, Idaho: Caxton Printers, 1965, pp. 121-125.

'Danger." *Rocky Mountain News,* December 16, 1891, p. 1, col. 1.

Rockwell, Wilson. *Memoirs of a Lawman*. Denver: Sage Books, 1962, pp. 233-257.

"The Strike Over." *Rocky Mountain News,* December 19, 1891, p. 1, col. 1.

"Terror." *Rocky Mountain News,* December 18, 1891, p. 1, col. 1.

"Under Fire." *Rocky Mountain News,* December 13, 1891, p. 1, col. 1.

Bob Ford posed with a Colt revolver. This photograph may have been taken after Ford killed Jesse James. The weapon he actually used to kill James was made by Smith & Wesson. *Western History Department, Denver Public Library*

Bob Ford Gunned Down in Creede

A n assassination plot to kill Jesse James might have begun when Missouri governor Thomas T. Crittenden put up a ten thousand dollar reward for the famous outlaw, dead or alive. In 1882, Jesse was living under the alias of Thomas Howard in St. Joseph, Missouri. Bob and Charley Ford were taken in by Jesse as new members of his gang. The Ford brothers were tempted by the large reward offered by the governor and remained with Jesse in an effort to catch him off guard.

On a warm spring day, Jesse opened the front door of his home to air it out. He thought it best to remove his revolvers lest the neighbors become suspicious. He stepped up on a chair to dust off a picture. This was just the kind of opportunity the Ford brothers were waiting for. They drew their revolvers, and as Jesse turned his head, Bob fired his Smith & Wesson .44-caliber revolver directly at Jesse, killing him instantly. Ironically, the revolver was a gift given to him by Jesse. The bullet entered the outlaw's forehead and exited the back of the head. Mrs. James rushed into the room and raised Jesse's head onto her lap. She tried to stop the flow of blood from the wound even though her Jesse was dead.

The Ford brothers rushed out of Jesse's home, wired the governor, then surrendered to the law for protection. They were indicted for first degree murder, pleaded guilty and were sentenced to be hanged. It was a strange turn of events for the brothers who viewed themselves as heroes for having rid Missouri of its most wanted criminal. Two hours later they were pardoned by the governor, but they were never able to collect their reward. In May 1884, Charley committed suicide. Bob Ford wandered to New Mexico, earning what he could by posing at dime museums.

Bob Ford ended up in Pueblo for a while, frequenting the saloons and gambling halls. It had been seven years since Jesse

James's death, but Bob's reputation followed him. The familiar song continued to haunt him wherever he went:

> Jesse had a wife
> She's a mourner all her life,
> Her children they are brave;
> Oh! the dirty little coward
> who shot Mister Howard
> And laid Jesse in his grave.[1]

Bob Ford moved to Walsenburg, Colorado, where he opened a combination saloon–gambling house. However, rumors of a new silver strike at Creede prompted Ford to close up and move to Creede. At the time, he was just twenty-eight years old and looked even younger than his years. Ford was a quiet man and seldom spoke unless asked a question.

In Creede, Bob Ford purchased a lot on the main street and constructed a two-story, rough, board building. He and his wife, Dot, lived upstairs and operated the Creede Exchange on the lower floor. The Exchange was a combination gambling and dancing hall. Ford ran the faro table and quickly became a favorite among Creede's lawless element. However, the sale of school land next to the Exchange forced Ford to close up shop in April 1892.

After the Exchange closed, Ford bet on a local prizefighter who was pitted against a professional named Johnson. The local fighter was beaten. Ford lost a great deal of money and began drinking. On the evening of Sunday, April 17, Ford and a companion planned to get even with Johnson by killing him. To get warmed up, they shot up Creede, breaking windows and narrowly missing several innocent bystanders. The prizefighter apparently left the area for his safety.

Enraged over this open display of lawlessness, some local citizens organized a secret society. Members called themselves the "One Hundred." A vote was taken, and the One Hundred elected to warn Ford and his companion rather than simply hanging them. The warning was delivered, and Ford left for Colorado Springs. While in the Springs, Bob Ford stated in an interview with one of the local newspapers, "I'm going back to Creede in a day or two with a gun in each hand." Ford later thought better of his threat against the town and in a few days wrote a number of Creede's businessmen stating he was sorry for what he did. He humbly asked for permission to return.

Ford returned to Creede April 27 and was greeted at the depot by many of his friends. He persuaded the editor of the *Morning Chronicle* to publish the following article:

> Bob Ford is again in Creede. Why the possibility of his return should have carried terror in the hearts of certain citizens is hardly possible to understand. Since he has been in Creede there has been no quieter man except on the unfortunate Sunday night a week ago. For this action upon that occasion he is extremely sorry, but after all, he displayed then the Western idea of staying by one's friends. . . . A fighting chance is all anyone wants and Ford should at least be granted that.

This editorial failed to satisfy the One Hundred, so Ford was forced to appear before the justice of the peace. He pleaded guilty to a misdemeanor and paid a fifty dollar fine. On the same evening that Ford's apology appeared in the *Chronicle*, Marshal Theodore Craig, representing the One Hundred, was asked to give Ford a second warning to leave town. Craig disagreed with the vigilante committee and refused to deliver the message.

All the publicity over this incident polarized the citizens of Creede either in favor of Ford or against him. His allies included contrasting members of Creede's society. For example, the town marshal and the justice of the peace were behind him. On the other hand, Jack Pugh (later killed by a local marshal) and Broken Nose Creek (a cousin of the Younger brothers) were also behind Ford. Because of the hostility of those who were against him, however, Ford threatened to burn the town to the ground. In spite of growing resentment, Ford stayed in Creede and opened a new dance hall on May 30, 1892.

In June, a fire started by a couple of drunks leveled much of the business district, and the One Hundred immediately thought Ford had put the drunks up to the job. As a result of the fire, Ford was left without a place of business. He erected a large tent and divided it into a combination dance hall and bar, with the living quarters in the rear. Although very primitive, the place was the only dance hall in Creede at the time, and it was well patronized.

Edward O. Kelly[2] was from Missouri, the son of a physician. He married a relative of the notorious Younger brothers, and it may have been through his wife that he knew the James family.[3] After his marriage, Ed Kelly drifted to Pueblo, Colorado. Here he worked on the police force but was eventually suspended. He also worked as a motorman on the town's street-railway system. Although there are a number of stories about how Ed Kelly first met Bob Ford, it may have been in a Pueblo hotel. A diamond ring belonging to Ford was stolen one night, and Kelly was blamed.[4]

In 1891, Ed O. Kelly shot and killed a Negro named Riley in an argument that began when Riley accidentally stepped on Kelly's toes. Kelly was somehow cleared of a murder charge and moved from Pueblo to the boomtown of Creede. In April 1892, he was elected town marshal of nearby Bachelor City. Following this stint as Bachelor City's marshal, he was made deputy sheriff of Hinsdale County.[5]

On June 8, 1892, a day after Ford's dance hall opened, Edward O. Kelly stood at the door talking to one of the women who worked in the dance hall. Joe Duval, also known as "French Joe," came riding down the street and quickly handed Kelly a loaded shotgun.[6] Ford was standing at the bar and was busy working on a subscription to raise money to bury Nellie Russell, who had worked for Ford and had died of an overdose of morphine.[7] Ford was busy obtaining signatures from his patrons when Kelly stepped into the tent. Ford started for the back of the room and Kelly followed closely. Kelly then said, "Oh, Bob!" Ford instinctively turned, dropping his hand to his revolver as Kelly discharged both barrels into Ford's head at point-blank range. His spinal cord was severed along with his jugular vein. The impact from the blast knocked Ford over backward. The floor was quickly covered with a great deal of blood, and Ford died almost instantly.

Deputy Sheriff Plunket, who was in the dance hall at the time, immediately arrested the killer. A lynch mob formed, and Ed Kelly was taken to a cabin some distance from town for his own safety.

Kelly was later transferred to the Rio Grande County jail. He refused to make any statements concerning the shooting. His case was heard on July 7, 1892, and he pleaded not guilty to second-degree murder. He was convicted and sentenced to life in

Edward O. Kelly was married to a relative of the notorious Younger brothers. Kelly shot Bob Ford to death in 1892. Kelly and Ford had met previously in Pueblo. Kelly was accused of stealing Ford's diamond ring. *Western History Collections, University of Oklahoma Library*

prison at the state penitentiary in Canon City. Clemency was sought, and his sentence was reduced to eighteen years. In 1902, Ed O. Kelly was pardoned and set free. He was killed in Oklahoma City two years later by a law officer.

Bob Ford had many friends in Creede. The funeral may have been the largest in Creede's history. The service was conducted by Rev. Davis in the People's Tabernacle on June 11, 1892. Cy Warman, then editor of the Creede *Chronicle*, commented that Rev. Davis was not very enthusiastic, but "he had a tough client and a hard case." At Ford's service, Rev. Davis talked about how charity covered a multitude of sins and he made the most of it. This was said to be the first funeral in Creede conducted with all the rites.

The casket was placed in the back of a wagon and taken up the steep, twisting road to the cemetery. Ford's widow later claimed the body and took it to Cass County, Missouri, for reburial. It is said that Dot Ford returned to Creede and became an entertainer at the Grand Theater.

Notes

1. The exact lyrics for this song vary somewhat among authors of western history. Another version is as follows:

> Jesse leaves a wife to mourn all her life,
> His children they were three.
> But the dirty little coward who shot Mr. Howard,
> He laid Jesse James in his grave.

2. Carl W. Breihan, in *The Complete and Authentic Life of Jesse James*, insists that his name was Edward O'Kelley; Bill O'Neal, in the *Encyclopedia of Western Gunfighters*, used Ed O. Kelly; and Nolie Mumey, in his book *Creede*, says the name was Ed O'Kelly. This author has used authority Raymon Adams and his book *Six-Guns and Saddle Leather* for the spelling Ed O. Kelly.

3. Historians disagree on the prior relationship between Kelly and the James gang.

4. There are a wide variety of accounts as to how Bob Ford and Ed Kelly met prior to Ford's death in Creede. In Frank C. Robertson and Beth Kay Harris's book, *Soapy Smith*, they say the two men had been rivals over the affections of a woman when the two were partners in a saloon in Walsenburg. They also say Kelly was an obscure member of

the James Gang. Carl W. Breihan, in his book *The Complete and Authentic Life of Jesse James,* says Ford pistol-whipped Kelly and took his gun. In this story, it is claimed that Kelly shot Ford to recover the weapon.

5. Other historians say Kelly served as marshal of Jimtown, another mining camp in the Creede area.

6. Some historical accounts say that Kelly had an accomplice, while others imply that he acted alone.

7. Accounts vary as to whether or not Nellie Russell actually worked for Ford or was simply another soiled dove. Her name also varies according to different accounts. In *Soapy Smith,* p. 104, she is referred to as Creede Lily.

References

Adams, Raymon F. *Six-Guns and Saddle Leather.* Norman, Okla.: University of Oklahoma Press, 1969, p. 159

Breihan, Carl W. *The Complete and Authentic Life of Jesse James.* New York: Frederick Fell, Inc., 1953, pp. 183–184, 189, 190.

Mumey, Nolie. *Creede.* Denver: Artcraft Press, 1949, pp. 135–148.

O'Neal, Bill. *Encyclopedia of Gunfighters.* Norman, Okla.: University of Oklahoma Press, 1979, p. 174.

Robertson, Frank C. and Beth Kay Harris. *Soapy Smith: King of the Frontier Con Men.* New York: Hastings House, 1961, pp. 110–134.

Creede, Colorado, around 1890. The town was located in a narrow canyon and during its heyday was one of the roughest mining camps in the state. *Colorado Historical Society*

Creede: A Town That Never Slept

C reede attracted all kinds of riff-raff that followed the prospectors and miners in the hope of profiting by their wealth. Every kind of business was profitable, but saloons and gambling halls were especially lucrative. Beer sold for twenty-five cents a glass, and whiskey ran as high as a dollar a drink during a time when wages were typically two dollars a day. There was so much demand for saloons and gambling halls that they opened in Creede and its neighboring towns in tents. A board across a couple of kegs served as the bar. At night, Creede changed into a carnival. Kerosene lamps and candles illuminated the saloons and dance halls around the clock, but recklessness was at an all-time high in the evening. Many miners worked all day for their silver riches only to leave them on the gaming tables at night. The meager law enforcement could not hope to keep up with Creede during its boom years.

Cy Warman founded the town's first newspaper, the Creede *Candle,* and celebrated the attractions of the town with the poem, "And There is No Night in Creede":

> Here's a land where all are equal—
> Of high or lowly birth—
> A land where men make millions,
> Dug from the dreary earth.
> Here meek and mild-eyed burros,
> On mineral mountains feed.
> It's day all day in the daytime,
> And there is no night in Creede.
> The cliffs are solid silver,
> With wond'rous wealth untold,
> And the beds of the running rivers
> Are lined with the purest gold.
> While the world is filled with sorrow,
> And the hearts must break and bleed—
> It's day all day in the daytime,
> And there is no night in Creede.

During 1891 and 1892, there were five murders in this rough town and a good many more non-fatal shootings.

In the early morning of March 31, 1892, a section of the main street of Creede was shot up. Bullets shattered windows on both sides of the street. The lives of those sleeping in second-story apartments were endangered. As a result of the disturbance, Deputy Marshal W. S. Light went to The Branch saloon. Here he found his suspect, "Reddy" McCann, a faro dealer from the Gunnison Exchange. McCann had been in Creede only six weeks, but had been involved in several altercations. Marshal Light tried to disarm McCann and, in the process, slapped McCann across the face, knocking a cigar out of his mouth.[1] At that moment, both reached for their guns, and five or six shots were fired in rapid succession. Patrons ducked behind the bar.

When the smoke cleared, Light walked away from the scene leaving Reddy McCann sprawled on the barroom floor. The bartender walked over to McCann, and the wounded man uttered the words, "I'm killed!" A doctor was summoned, and McCann was laid on a table. He died fifteen minutes after the shooting.

Marshal Light was a brother-in-law of one of the West's most famous con men, Soapy Smith. Light previously had served as marshal in Belden, Texas. He was not known as a quarrelsome man, and it was later determined at the coroner's inquest that he had acted in self-defense.

A second murder took place in Creede later that same day around 10:00 P.M. In the upper portion of the town, which was located in a narrow canyon, a man's voice shouted, "For God's sake, don't shoot!" A shot followed, with cries of pain and a woman's scream.

Billie Wall and his lady friend, Ella Diamond, had been on their way home. They stopped at a saloon (one of the thirty in Creede and its neighbor, Jimtown), and there they met Frank Oliver. Oliver was drunk, and the same could be said of Billie Wall. Oliver took another drink and stepped outside the saloon onto the sidewalk. Wall took one last drink with the saloon's owner and left with Ella Diamond guiding him down the street. Once outside, Wall began to vomit from all the liquor he had consumed. At the same time, Frank Oliver directed abusive language at Wall. Ella begged Oliver to leave them alone.

Without warning, Oliver drew his gun and fired at the helpless Wall.

Wall collapsed in the street with a .38-caliber ball just below his heart. The ball traveled down into his vital organs. A couple of men grabbed Oliver until law officer Jack Pugh arrived to take charge of the prisoner. Wall was carried back into the saloon and laid out on one of the gaming tables. Dr. Logan, who happened to be passing by, went into do what he could for the wounded man, but Wall died around midnight. Ella Diamond was at his side all the time.

In July 1892, Frank Oliver was convicted of voluntary manslaughter and was sentenced to the state penitentiary in Canon City for a six-year term.

Jack Pugh was a noted Colorado character. He was a neat-looking man and well educated. He came to Creede in 1891 and established a livery stable, but he was soon the first commissioned deputy sheriff in Upper Creede. When sober, Pugh was very likeable, but when drunk he was mean. In November 1891, he was involved in one of the town's earliest shootings. Pugh and a friend, Jack Fullerton, shot up the McLeod Saloon, operated by Jack Ferris. Ferris was forced to flee his own business for fear of being killed. The following day, Ferris sought revenge and hid behind a building. When Pugh and Fullerton were crossing one of the bridges in town, Ferris opened fire. Fullerton was hit in the shoulder, and a ball cut through Pugh's clothing without touching him. Ferris fled down the trail that paralleled the Rio Grande River, then traveled north across the San Luis Valley to Saguache. Here he gave himself up to the local authorities and waited. Much to his surprise, no one filed charges, and he was released.

Jack Pugh later hit an innocent spectator in the foot during another shooting. Because of his itchy trigger finger and unpredictable nature, he had a reputation for being able to empty a saloon faster than any man in Creede.

In January 1892, Pugh "jumped" a lot belonging to Mayor and Mrs. F. M. Osgood. He hired some men to place lumber on the lot and to hold it. Mrs. Osgood was away from Creede at the time but heard of Pugh's illegal action. She returned and recaptured the lot using hired men to throw the lumber aside. As she stood guard, the men quickly constructed a frame building.

Mayor Osgood operated the Holy Moses saloon (named for Nicholas C. Creede's Holy Moses silver mine, which got the town of Creede started). Four months after the attempt to steal the Osgood lot, Jack Pugh entered the establishment. After drinking all day long, he had become exceedingly mean and unruly. The Holy Moses sat on the very same lot that Pugh had tried to steal. At around five o'clock, Pugh began talking about revenge, and Mayor Osgood knew that Pugh was after him. He laid his gun on a nearby table, fearing Jack would make trouble.

Jack was playing seven-up and drinking heavily. Marshal Karg entered the saloon, and Osgood asked him to stay for a while to keep an eye on Pugh. By around ten o'clock, Jack was louder than ever, and the marshal asked him to quiet down. The marshal also told him he was drunk and ought to go home. Karg talked to Pugh in a quiet tone of voice, but Pugh wanted to fight. Pugh took hold of the marshal and spun him around, saying that Karg could not arrest him. He threatened to kill Karg if he tried. Karg quickly called for help, broke loose from Pugh's grip, and ran to the rear of the saloon. Pugh drew his gun and started after the law officer, yelling, "You damn Dutch son of a bitch, I'll kill you." Karg drew, fired, and shot Jack Pugh on the spot.

Pugh collapsed near the stove used to heat the saloon and an hour later was carried to his home. The shooting took place at 1:30 A.M., and Pugh talked rationally up to the time of his death at 6:15 A.M. He was buried at Del Norte, and his mistress, Lillian Shields, was the only person to accompany the body. She later related that this was Pugh's second visit to the Holy Moses to kill Mayor Osgood.

Jurisdiction problems complicated the inquests. One inquest had to be held in Jimtown and another in Upper Creede because the Holy Moses saloon, where the shooting took place, was located in Saguache County, but Pugh's home was in Hinsdale County. Both juries returned the verdict that the killing was justifiable.

Lillian Shields charged Marshal Karg with her common-law husband's murder. Karg had been born in Germany, lived in Kansas City, and then moved to Creede. He had become town marshal only three weeks prior to the shooting. His case was postponed twice, and in the meantime, he resigned his position as marshal and moved out of the area.

William Rumidge had been Lillie's lover prior to Jack Pugh. After Jack's death, Lillie returned to Rumidge. On May 24, 1892, Lillie and Rumidge were in the Junction Saloon drinking and playing cards. Rumidge kept teasing Lillie about the way she was playing. She finally became so angry she drew her gun, fired, and fatally wounded her lover. Rumidge was carried to the same house and placed on the same bed where Jack Pugh had died just three weeks earlier. Rumidge died at noon on May 25. Lillie's case was heard, and possibly because she was a woman, she was set free.

Almost a month went by in Creede without any serious shootings, then Sheriff Soufa was asked to quiet Thomas Coyne and his three or four companions. The men had been drinking all day at one of the dance halls. The sheriff ended up putting handcuffs on Coyne, but one of Coyne's friends, a man named McCoy, broke the chains and helped Coyne escape.

The sheriff caught up with McCoy and took him into custody. Bill Hogue was deputized to arrest Thomas Coyne. Armed with a shotgun, Hogue followed Coyne to his cabin and attempted to arrest him. Coyne resisted, and Hogue immediately emptied both barrels into the man. One load of shot penetrated Coyne's hip, and the other grazed his head.

When Coyne's friends learned of the shooting, they set out after Hogue with a rope. Hogue defended himself well by clubbing a few of the men and holding the rest at bay with a revolver in each hand. He escaped from the mob and left Creede, never to return. Coyne died from his wounds.

Like other mining towns in Colorado, Creede was a community born in violence. But eventually, as law and order moved west into the mountains, it and the other boomtowns were tamed.

Notes

1. This incident is told according to an account published in the Creede *Candle*, April 1, 1892.

References

Hansen, Harry, ed. *Colorado: A Guide to the Highest State.* New York: Hastings House, 1970, p. 240.

Mumey, Nolie. *Creede.* Denver: Artcraft Press, 1949, pp. 95-118.

Creede *Candle,* April 1, 1892, p. 1, col. 3.

Hardware store owner Ray Simpson shot two of the members of the McCarty gang to death after the robbery of the Farmers & Merchants Bank in Delta. He used a Sharps .44-caliber rifle. *Drawn by Kenneth Jessen*

The End of the McCarty Gang

T om McCarty was born in 1841. His father, Dr. William McCarty, served in the Civil War as a Confederate surgeon. After the war ended, the family moved to Montana. In 1871, the McCartys moved again, this time to Grass Valley, Utah.

By 1884, Tom and his brother Bill sold their Utah ranch for $35,000. Tom gambled away his share, then turned his attention to horse stealing. He married Tennie Christiansen, sister of Matt Warner. Warner became a well-known Utah outlaw, and Tom joined him for some bank jobs.

Bill, on the other hand, abandoned his wife, Letty, and married a young girl. He neglected to tell his new bride that he was already married. He and his second wife moved to Oregon.

Eventually, Tom got caught red handed near Nephi, Utah, with some stolen stock. His father-in-law put up bail, but Tom failed to appear in court and fled into the Blue (Abajo) Mountains of Utah. Here he headed a successful gang of rustlers. Tom had a busy schedule ranging from rustling to armed robbery. He was even hired at times by unsuspecting ranchers to recover the very horses he had stolen.

In March 1889, Tom made an appointment with David Moffat, president of the First National Bank of Denver and one of Colorado's richest men. On March 30, Tom met Moffat in his private office just off the main banking rooms. He began talking to Moffat about how his bank was going to be robbed. Just when he had Moffat interested, Tom exclaimed, "I am the man who is going to rob your bank." At the same time, he drew a revolver and began to act crazy. He told Moffat he was a desperate man and had decided to kill himself the night before. He changed his mind and came to rob the bank instead. He then carefully lifted a bottle of clear liquid out of his topcoat. Tom told the astonished Moffat it was nitroglycerine. He said

David Moffat, one of Colorado's richest men, was one of Tom McCarty's robbery victims. Moffat, while in his office in Denver's First National Bank, was forced to turn over twenty-one-thousand dollars to Tom McCarty. McCarty pretended to hold a bottle of nitroglycerine and threatened to blow up the bank if Moffat failed to comply. *Colorado Historical Society*

he would use it to blow up the bank and everyone in it unless Moffat wrote out a check for twenty-one thousand dollars and had it cashed in his own bank. Tom continued to act insane and did it so well that Moffat wrote out the check.

The cashier had to be told twice to cash the check but finally brought in the money. There was one thousand dollars in gold and the rest in currency. Tom continued to act like a crazy man. As he left the bank, he passed the money, without being noticed, to Ras Christenson who was stationed by the bank door. The two men fled in opposite directions. McCarty took a hack back to the his hotel and, once in his room, changed into a black minister's suit. Ras walked calmly away from the bank and was soon lost in the crowd. Tom remained in Denver for a week then joined Ras in Star Valley, Wyoming, to split the loot.

The cashier, however, had slipped a ten thousand dollar bill in with the cash. The bill could be easily identified by a missing corner. All law officers in the Rocky Mountain region were notified to look out for the bill. But as time passed, the bill failed to show up. It can be assumed that this portion of the money was never spent in the Rocky Mountain region.

At ten o'clock in the morning, June 24, 1889, the San Miguel Valley Bank in Telluride was held up and robbed of twenty-four thousand dollars. The three bandits were Tom McCarty, Matt Warner, and Butch Cassidy. Two of the bandits entered the bank while the third sat on his horse in front of the entrance holding his companions' horses. While in the bank, the robbers told assistant cashier C. L. Hyde and others not to sound any alarm for at least ten minutes. After the holdup, the men galloped west down Main Street shooting their revolvers in the air.

Harry Adsit, a cattleman from the nearby Norwood area, saw the three outlaws gallop out of town toward San Miguel City. He joined Sheriff J. A. Beattie and the posse. Adsit had a faster horse and rode far ahead of the posse.

Somewhere between Telluride and Rico, Tom McCarty hid behind a rock. The outlaw must have sensed that the law was getting a little too close for comfort. When Adsit approached, McCarty jumped out and used his gun to relieve Adsit of his pearl-handled six-shooter. He told him not to get close again or he would kill him.[1]

In a style that characterized Butch Cassidy, the three robbers had fresh horses waiting between Rico and Dolores. They changed horses and drove their first set of mounts ahead of them—except for one horse that was too tired to go on. When the posse arrived, Sheriff Beattie took the horse with him and rode it around Telluride for many years afterward.

At one point during the chase, the posse got close to the robbers. Matt Warner spied a pony, roped the animal, then tied a bush to its tail. He sent the animal galloping toward the posse. The dust raised by the dragging bush and the noise of the frightened animal crashing toward them disrupted the chase, and the outlaws escaped.

After the Telluride robbery, Tom McCarty turned his attention to the banks in Oregon. He robbed $3,450 from the Oregon National Bank in Walla Walla on October 8, 1891, then took $5,000 from the Farmers Mortgage & Savings Bank in Summerville a month later.

Colorado, however, had not seen the last of the McCartys. On September 7, 1893, three men rode down the alley behind the Farmers & Merchants Bank in Delta. The bank had been founded by Andrew T. Blachly and one other man. It was situated on the east side of Main Street, a few doors south of Third Street. One of the men held the horses while the other two walked up the sidewalk, around the north side of the building, then inside.

It was a little after ten o'clock in the morning, and the bank had just opened its doors. The safe was open so that money could be placed on the counter to handle the day's business. Andrew Blachly, cashier, was busy typing, and H. H. Wolbert, assistant cashier, was working at a desk.

As the strangers approached the cashier's window, Blachly got up to wait on them. Suddenly, the two men drew their revolvers and covered Blachly and Wolbert. One of the bank robbers was a short, beardless youth of about eighteen. He was dressed in a dark coat and blue overalls and wore low-cut shoes. He was Fred McCarty, son of Bill McCarty. His father was the other man with the gun. Bill was around forty, about five-foot-ten-inches tall and was powerfully built. He had a sandy mustache and a straggley beard. There was a certain family resemblance between the two men.

On September 7, 1893, Bill McCarty, his son Fred, and Bill's brother
Tom attempted to hold up the Farmers & Merchants Bank in Delta.
Hardware store owner Ray Simpson blew the top of Bill's head off with
his Sharps .44-caliber rifle when the outlaw tried to ride out of town.
Colorado Historical Society

Cashier Blachly refused to cooperate with the robbers in handing over the bank's money. Fred McCarty jumped up on the counter at the cashier's window. Blachly reacted by shouting for help. Assistant Cashier Wolbert stooped to reach for his gun, and Fred yelled from the counter, "Lay down that gun." Blachly was told to shut up or his head would be blown off. As the money was being handed out through the cashier's window by Fred to his father, Blachly again shouted for help. Fred fired twice. One of the bullets pierced the top of his head, killing him instantly. The other bullet crashed into the floor.[2]

Realizing that the shots would be heard outside on Delta's main street, the outlaws took time only to stuff their pockets with what bills and coins they could grab. A bag of gold was snatched out of the safe, and the robbers fled out the rear door, taking Wolbert with them.

In the alley, they found their partner with his six-shooter pointed at W. R. Robertson, a Delta attorney. Robertson had been in the rear of the bank when Fred killed the cashier. He rushed out the back door where he met the third outlaw holding the horses. This man was none other than Tom McCarty.

The three outlaws mounted their horses and spurred them into a full gallop. They headed north down the alley. In their haste, they left the bag of gold behind on the ground.

Ray Simpson, junior owner of the hardware store of W. G. Simpson & Son, was cleaning his Sharps .44-caliber rifle at the time of the bank robbery. The hardware store was directly across Main Street from the bank. Simpson was thirty-one, a tall and slender man. He loved to hunt and was a crack shot. He was quiet, cool, and calm.

Upon hearing the two shots from the interior of the bank, Simpson quickly pulled the lever down on the Sharps to drop the breech block. He inserted a shell and grabbed several more as he ran out of the store. He went over to the corner of Third and Main, then east on Third to the alley. Just then, he saw the outlaws coming at a full gallop down the alley. Simpson fired from the hip at the man in the rear, Bill McCarty. The entire top of Bill's head was blown off, and his brains ended up some twenty feet from where he fell from his horse. Simpson dropped the breech block again to insert another shell.

In the meantime, young Fred McCarty pulled up to see if he could help his fallen father. Fred was nearly a block away from Simpson, but that moment of hesitation gave Simpson a clear shot. The bullet from Simpson's rifle hit Fred in the base of the skull, then came out his forehead. Tom McCarty did not slow to see what had happened to his brother or nephew, but continued to ride hard. Money from the robbery was scattered in all directions in the street.

Simpson fired again, this time at Tom, but the bullet hit one of the riderless horses. The wounded animal returned to Third Street, where it fell dead. Simpson fired a second round at Tom McCarty just as he turned down Second Street, but the bullet missed.

Delta sheriff Girardet was sitting in the office of the Delta *Independent* on the corner of Fourth and Main when the holdup occurred. When he found out what had happened, he mounted his horse and, accompanied by Ray Simpson and several other men, chased the one remaining bandit. Tom, however, had placed fresh horses along his route and was able to out-distance the posse. A five hundred dollar reward was put up for his capture but never collected.

Later during the day of the bank robbery, the two dead outlaws were propped up against a barn. Photographs were taken, but Bill's hat was placed on his head to cover the fact that the top of his head was missing. These photos were distributed in an effort to identify the dead men. A man by the name of Taylor came from Moab, Utah. He was an uncle by marriage of Bill McCarty and identified the outlaws. Ex-Denver Police Chief Farley came from Denver and also identified the dead men. Farley had been tracking Tom McCarty ever since he held up the First National Bank in Denver.

Simpson began receiving letters from Tom McCarty threatening to kill him, his wife, and their three daughters. For months, the notes kept coming in until Simpson could no longer take it. He was forced to leave Delta and start his life all over. Simpson died at the age of seventy-eight and is buried in the famous Forest Lawn cemetery in Glendale, California.[3]

Mrs. Blachly, the wife of the slain cashier, was left to raise eight boys by herself. She was a cultured, college-trained woman and gave music lessons to support her family. She managed to put all of her boys through college.

Fred McCarty, son of Bill McCarty, killed cashier Andrew T. Blachly and was then shot to death by Ray Simpson when he attempted to escape from Delta. The bullet entered the base of Fred's skull, killing him instantly. *Colorado Historical Society*

Tom McCarty hid out for some time on a mesa above La Sal Creek in western Montrose County. His relatives and friends in Paradox Valley brought him food and supplies. Stories vary as to what ultimately happened to Tom McCarty after the Delta holdup, but one possibility is that he went to Oregon and established a horse ranch.[4] The death of his brother and nephew seemed to take the starch out of him.

Notes

1. Adsit's own account varies materially. He admitted leading the posse at a slow pace, even stopping for a half hour at one point. Adsit's version has him staying with the posse during the chase. Apparently the posse could have caught up with the three outlaws at Trout Lake, but didn't try.

2. Accounts vary as to how many times Blachly was shot. For example, in Richard Churchill's book, *The McCartys,* p. 36, he says Blachly was shot twice in the head.

3. Churchill says that Simpson responded to one of Tom McCarty's threatening letters by sending the outlaw a card with ten tightly grouped bullet holes in it made with his new Winchester at 225 feet. If Simpson knew McCarty's address, however, it is puzzling that the outlaw wasn't arrested.

4. Roy O'Dell of Cambridge, England, an expert on the outlaws of the American West, states, "Concerning the death of Tom McCarty, there are numerous accounts. Pointer states *(In Search of Butch Cassidy)* Tom abandoned the outlaw life, drifting to Montana. He eventually settled near Rosebud, Montana (see *True West,* Nov. 1984, 'Answer Man' p. 17). Some reports state that Tom was killed near Green River, Utah. Matt Warner had said that he believed Tom to have been killed in Montana's Bitterroot Valley. Also there are reports that Tom went to Skagway, Alaska, during the gold rush and was killed or died there. Others say that he was living in the Enterprise, Oregon, area as late as 1912. *The Mysterious Pinkerton* by Kerry Ross Boren states that Tom went to Alaska in 1900 where he was killed two years later. Skovin, in *The McCarty Gang,* states that Tom may have gone to Utah after the ill-fated robbery at Delta, Colorado. Other reports state he was in Montana or Oregon. He may have been stealing horses out from his McCarty Springs Ranch in Utah as late as 1905."

References

Burroughs, John Rolfe. *Where the Old West Stayed Young*. New York: Bonanza Books, 1962, pp. 119-123.

Churchill, Richard. *The McCartys—They Rode with Butch Cassidy*. Leadville, Colo.: Timberline Books, 1972.

"Daring Bandits." *Rocky Mountain News*, September 8, 1893, p. 1, col. 1.

"M'Carthy's [sic] Gang." *Rocky Mountain News*, September 11, 1893, p. 1, col. 1.

O'Neal, Bill. *Encyclopedia of Western Gunfighters*. Norman, Okla.: University of Oklahoma Press, 1979, pp. 203, 204.

Rockwell, Wilson. *Uncompahgre Country*. Denver: Sage Books, 1965, pp. 41-48, 288-289.

———. *Sunset Slope*. Denver: Big Mountain Press, 1956, pp. 67-79.

"Still on the Chase." *Rocky Mountain News*, September 9, 1893, p. 2, col. 2.

KENNETH JESSEN

Queen of the Red-Light District

B eginning in 1875, men and a few women poured into the
Lake City area with boundless optimism for the future.
Miners arrived without a mine to work, and merchants came
without stock to sell. People came and went, leaving behind
very little in the way of memorials to their contributions. But
occasionally an individual left behind an account of his or her
lifestyle.

Miss Clara Ogden was a denizen of Lake City's red-light
district on Bluff Street. She was a highly successful manager of
her type of business at a time when people were glad to have
crystal and illusion momentarily replace the hard reality of
living in this remote San Juan town. Clara Ogden brought a
new style to Lake City by clearing away some of the shabby
cribs that lined Bluff Street. She erected the Crystal Palace, a
dance hall and bordello of extraordinary quality. It included a
second story with a score of bedrooms. On the ground floor
were parlors and a ballroom. Crystal chandeliers, mirrors, and
thick carpeting helped to create the illusion of grandeur; walnut
and mahogany furniture filled the structure.

By 1894, Clara had risen to the top of her profession as head
madam of the district. Typically, young women arriving in the
area looking for a job or a husband were helped by the madam.
Soon the women would find themselves in debt for lodging and
clothing. This allowed Clara to demand repayment by forcing
the women to work in her brothel.

Teenage boys were sometimes attracted to these young women
for their first sexual experiences. In the November 29, 1894,
issue of the Lake City *Times,* the following notice appeared:

! NOTICE !

Notice is hereby given boys under the age of twenty-one, that it
is strictly against the law for them to visit saloons or houses of ill

fame. Considerable complaint has been made to me from owners of sporting houses in regard to minors frequenting their places, and I hereby give notice that I will hereafter enforce the law in this respect. Fair warning—I will treat all alike.

Joe B. Michaels
City Marshal

Seeking to expand her already successful business, during the early part of 1895 Clara Ogden looked at some of the neighboring mining camps, including Capitol City, Carson, and Sherman. Entertainment of the type she offered wasn't available at these locations, and she envisioned a chain of brothels. The first step was the purchase of an elegant carriage pulled by matched bay horses. Weekly, Clara would load up her women and head out for a day's outing in the mountains. The women were asked to do no more than look attractive. Clara never did set up a branch operation, but she did a lot of advertising by showing off the "merchandise."

In 1895, the prosperity in Lake City began its inevitable decline as the mines played out and the ore became harder to reach deep inside the mountains. Tension began to build; few people had steady work. Street brawls and shootings prompted local law officers to strengthen city ordinances concerning saloon hours and the Bluff Street trade. As the mood of her patrons became less optimistic about the future, however, Clara's business increased, and she began her most elegant and showy days as a hostess. The old upright piano was replaced with a concert grand. The latest rags were played, and her grand ballroom was often filled to capacity.

On the night of June 11, 1896, Clara Ogden was dressed in one of her many Paris gowns. She was serving drinks to her patrons as piano music rose above the sound of laughter. Suddenly there were shots and screams. The illusion created within the Crystal Palace was shattered.

Louis Estep and Frank McDonald had been standing in the door leading to the grand ballroom. One of Clara's women, Jessie Landers, came out of her room and fired at McDonald. Instead of hitting its target, the bullet struck Estep in back of the ear, killing him instantly. McDonald ran down the hall as the woman fired twice at him. Both rounds missed. Jessie then ran outside and shot herself in the left breast. The bullet passed through her body, coming out her side.

Louis Estep was around twenty-two years old and was the only son of his widowed mother. Estep and Jessie were engaged to be married, and when she saw her finance with Frank McDonald, a known pimp, she opened fire.

Jessie survived her wound and stood trial. Judge Gabbert gave the jury and courtroom audience a few touching words about the nature of the crime and the continuing tragedy of the women who made their livings as prostitutes. Clara Ogden circulated a petition asking that Jessie be given the minimum sentence. Jessie pleaded guilty to voluntary manslaughter and was sentenced to five years in the state penitentiary in Canon City.

The shooting death of Louis Estep spelled the end of Lake City's red-light district. Clara extinguished the lamps and chandeliers in the Crystal Palace and vanished, never to be seen again in Lake City. The abandoned building stood for several years, then caught fire. What was once the center of entertainment in Lake City was reduced to ashes.

In an effort to clean up the town in 1898, Lake City passed the following ordinance:

Any person who shall keep a bawdy house, house of ill fame, assignation house, a house for promiscuous dancing, commonly called a dance house, or a disorderly house of any description whatever, within the limits of the town of Lake City, or within three miles of the outer limit thereof . . . suffer to permit any drunkenness, quarreling, fighting, unlawful gambling or disorderly conduct whatever on or in his or her premises, shall be subject to a fine of not less than five ($5) nor more than one hundred ($100) dollars for each offense.

This, once and for all, put an end to the business on Bluff Street.

References

Houston, Grant. *Lake City Reflections*. Gunnison, Colo.: B. & B. Printers, 1976, pp. 85-94.

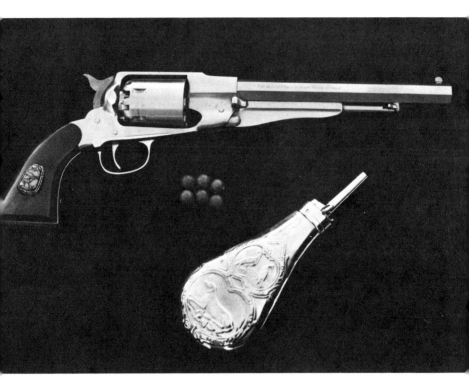

Meeker Citizens Rally to Stop Bank Robbers

J. W. Hagus owned a mercantile store in Meeker. The Bank of Meeker had its offices in that store at one end of the building. The Hagus store was more than one hundred feet deep and was located at the corner of Main and Sixth streets. On Main Street was the main entrance to the store. A side door along Sixth Street provided access to the bank and a secondary entrance to the store. Opposite the side entrance were a number of wagon sheds.

An attempted robbery of the Bank of Meeker took place October 13, 1896, in broad daylight. It was one of the most daring ever perpetrated in the West.

At around 2:30 P.M., the three men entered the store, one through the side door and the other two through the front door. Joe Rooney, a clerk at the Meeker Hotel, had stepped into the bank to make a deposit and stood talking to assistant cashier David Smith. As Rooney turned to leave, he felt a heavy hand on his shoulder. Glancing up, he found himself looking into the muzzle of a revolver. The man with the revolver commanded, "Hands up!" Smith hesitated and the man fired a shot past his head. Still slow to respond, he felt a second bullet whiz by his head, causing him to raise his hands instantly.

In the meantime, the other two robbers covered the people in the store and forced them to move to the center of the room. The customers and store employees were disarmed. The robbers gathered what guns and cartridges they wanted.

Cashier Moulton was called out from the banking room and forced at gunpoint to open the safe. In the safe's drawer was seven hundred dollars in cash, which was quickly stuffed into a sack. Not a word was spoken by any of the men as they worked. They went about their business with a deliberation that was astounding under the conditions.

When they had what they wanted, one of the robbers announced to the crowd in the store that their horses were outside in one of the wagon sheds and that they wanted everyone to march out the side door single file ahead of them in case there was trouble. The customers, store clerks, and bank employees immediately left through the door. As soon as they began to emerge, they realized their fellow citizens had surrounded the building. From behind the sheds, they could see rifle barrels. Other Meeker residents held pistols and shotguns. As the store occupants left through the side door, they gave no indication of the situation, so as the three robbers stepped out onto the street, it became a matter of surrendering or fighting.

When the warning shots had been fired during the holdup, Deputy Game Warden W. H. Clark saw three horses tied up in one of the wagon sheds. Realizing that something was wrong inside the store, he gathered up as many men as he could and placed them around the side door. He also put several other men near the front door.

The leader of the robbers, using a rifle he had taken from inside the store, fired at Clark, striking him in the left breast only an inch or so from the lung. At that, a volley of shots rang out from a dozen directions, obscuring the scene with gunsmoke. In the deadly cross fire, two of the robbers crumpled to the ground, their chests riddled with bullets. Any one of their wounds would have proved fatal. The third robber, the youngest, was struck several times, but continued to fire. He staggered down Sixth Street and fell at the intersection with Market.

The lone survivor lived about an hour and a half, giving his name as George Harris and those of his companions as Charles Jones and William Smith. He cried out, "Oh, mother!" just before he died.

On October 19, the *Rocky Mountain News* delivered this heart-rending analysis:

Somewhere in this broad land there is a woman who is wondering why she does not hear from her boy, and knows not that he is resting in a dishonored grave on the banks of (the) White River. It may be well, perhaps, if she never learns of his fate, for then she will never think of him as one of the trio who fell before the avenging bullets of Meeker's citizens. The loving kindness of

In the foreground lies the body of Jim Shirley. In the background, behind the trees, is the body of George Law. These two men and Billy Smith were shot to death by angered Meeker citizens when they attempted to rob the Meeker bank. *Colorado Historical Society*

his mother; her lessons, her advice, her prayers, must have flashed across the mind of the dying boy, as he lay in his death agony, and to save her the disgrace of his unfortunate career, he died without revealing his true name.

The dead men were removed to an undertaker. An inquest produced a verdict of justifiable homicide. Photographs were taken of the dead bank robbers and distributed to law enforcement agencies. At first it was believed that Tom McCarty was the gang leader, but the job was far too sloppy. Finally on October 25, two men from Brown's Hole arrived in Meeker. They claimed the horses and identified the dead robbers as Billy Smith (the young boy), George Law, and Jim Shirley. George Law was a nephew of a long-time resident and store owner in Brown's Hole by the same name. Smith was from Johnson County, Wyoming.

In addition to Game Warden Clark being wounded, Victor Dikeman was shot in the left arm, C. A. Booth received a scalp wound near the ear, and W. P. Herrick had a finger shot off. This was the last time armed bank robbery was attempted in Meeker during the 1800s.

References

"Bandits Not Dead." *Rocky Mountain News*, October 18, 1896, p. 1, col. 6.

"Desperadoes Were at Work." Colorado Springs *Gazette*, p. 1, col. 4.

"Filled Them with Lead." *Grand Junction Weekly Star-Times*, October 17, 1896, p. 1, col. 1.

"Letter from Meeker." *Rocky Mountain News*, October 17, 1896, p. 2, col. 5.

"Meeker's Dead Robbers." *Rocky Mountain News*, October 16, 1896, p. 2, col. 4.

"A Pathetic Incident." *Rocky Mountain News*, October 19, 1896, p. 2, col. 4.

Patterson, Richard. *Historical Atlas of the Outlaw West*. Boulder: Johnson Books, 1985, pp. 43-44.

"The Robbers Identified." Grand Junction *Weekly Star-Times,* October 31, 1896, p. 1, col. 2.

Rockwell, Wilson. *Sunset Slope.* Denver: Bib Mountain Press, 1956, pp. 80–92.

"Three Bank Robbers Killed at Meeker." *Rocky Mountain News,* October 15, 1896, p. 1, col. 1.

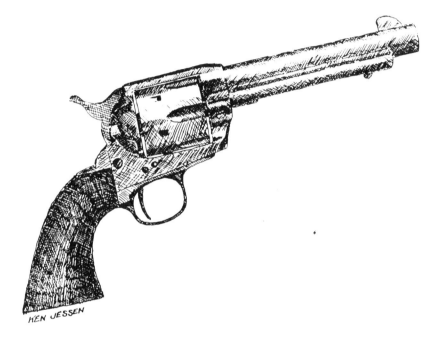

KEN JESSEN

Epilogue

The stories presented in *Colorado Gunsmoke* represent only a few of the pre-1900 gunfights in the state. To tantalize the reader into more reading, a few other interesting events are presented in this epilogue.

Denver was the scene of such violence during its first few years that it is difficult to know where to begin. Auraria and Denver, located on opposite sides of Cherry Creek, were rivals. Peleg Bassett and John Scudder were former Missouri riverboat pilots and long-time friends. They ended up, however, on opposite sides of Cherry Creek with Bassett serving as Denver's first recorder; Scudder was the treasurer of Auraria.

The two men constantly argued over the merits of their respective towns. One of the their disagreements developed in the middle of Larimer Street on April 16, 1859. Bassett reached for a pick handle and lunged at Scudder. The Auraria man leaped out of the way, drew his gun, and fired at his former friend. The ball caught Bassett in the chest, and he died about eight hours later. Scudder felt it best to leave the area to avoid sudden justice at the end of a rope.

Richard E. Whitsitt succeeded Peleg Bassett as Denver recorder. A man named Park McClure claimed Whitsitt had been spreading lies about him and asked the mayor of Denver to draft a formal challenge to a duel. McClure was hotheaded and loved a good quarrel. Whitsitt was just the opposite; he was tall, distinguished, and soft-spoken.

When the gauntlet had been flung in the form of an official paper, the weapons were selected: Navy Colts, to be fired at ten paces. The duel took place on October 18, 1859, at 5:30 in the evening along the banks of Cherry Creek, about a mile out of Denver. As the first shots were to be fired at virtually point-blank range, the likelihood of a casualty was high. For this reason, the event attracted more than five hundred people. McClure was an expert marksman; Whitsitt feared guns.

At the count of five, both men turned and fired simultaneously. Whitsitt closed his eyes as he pulled the trigger. Both men stood motionless as the gunsmoke cleared, then McClure toppled over with a bullet in the groin. Whitsitt was uninjured. Fortunately, McClure later recovered from his wound.

A common expression in the Rocky Mountain region for a cemetery was "O'Neil's Ranch." The term originated when Jack O'Neil was killed by John Rooker. O'Neil got into an argument during a poker game with Rooker on March 29, 1860. The disagreement took place in Dick Wooton's Western Saloon on Ferry Street. Both O'Neil and Rooker left the establishment and went their own ways. The following morning, when the saloon was closed, Rooker slipped into the building through an unlocked rear door. He hid so he could see Ferry Street through the front windows. Jack O'Neil lived on Ferry Street, and Rooker knew he would eventually come into view. Sure enough, around ten o'clock, O'Neil walked down the street from his residence toward a hardware store to pick up some nails. As he passed the saloon, Rooker discharged both barrels of his shotgun at O'Neil. As O'Neil fell, he tried in vain to draw one of his revolvers. Rooker rode out of town to escape the law, and O'Neil died of his wounds.[1]

The present-day settlement of Beulah is located in a valley known as Mace's Hole. It was once the hideout of Juan Mace, a Mexican outlaw. The only entrance into Mace's Hole is through a narrow pass. Local cattlemen knew Juan Mace was stealing their cattle, but they didn't dare enter the valley for fear of being ambushed. One day in the summer of 1863, Juan Mace was caught alone on the prairie, far from the safety of his hideout. He was gunned down there by some of the cattlemen.[2]

On August 25, 1877, at Denver's Olympic Gardens, what might be the only duel between female adversaries in the history of Colorado took place. Mattie Silks and Katie Fulton, well-known Denver prostitutes, got into an argument so great that only a duel could satisfy them. Seconds were selected, and the women stood back-to-back. When the count began, the two ladies of the evening walked away from each other. At the count of three, they turned and fired. A loud scream penetrated the air. Blood spurted from between the fingers of Cort Thompson, Mattie's male companion. The women had missed each other. Fortunately, Cort's wound was only superficial, and he later recovered.[3]

Gambler-gunfighter Luke Short visited Leadville in 1879. Although few details of the incident are available, it is known that he got into a gun battle with a man named Brown. The men fought over a gambling debt, and Brown was wounded in the face.[4]

In 1880, over the unfounded impression that his mistress had been seeing Clay Wilson, Jim Moon decided to hunt down Wilson. A man of violence, Moon often used his size, strength, and fists rather than a gun to beat his victims into submission. Moon found Wilson in a Denver tavern and attempted to taunt him into a fist fight. Wilson feared he would be killed and drew his revolver as Moon approached. When Moon was practically within reach, Wilson fired and struck the big man in the abdomen. This failed to slow Moon's advance as he grabbed Wilson's gun arm and tried to dislodge the weapon. Wilson used his free hand to bring the muzzle of his revolver around. He pulled on the barrel while holding the trigger, causing the gun to discharge and sending a bullet into Moon's body. This caused Moon to release his grip on Wilson. Just to make certain of Moon's fate, Wilson fired once more as Moon slumped to the barroom floor and died at Wilson's feet.[5]

Bill Miner, alias Old Bill, The Gentleman Bandit, Bill Morgan, George Anderson, Bill Anderson, George Edwards, and The Gray Fox, spent nearly all of his life, from 1863 to 1911, robbing stagecoaches and trains. Bill Miner was five-feet-eleven-inches tall, weighed 140 pounds, had a large mustache and blue eyes, and was considered good looking by the ladies. He is said to have originated the command, "Hands up!" used by so many outlaws and lawmen after him. Always courteous and soft spoken, Miner was an expert shot. Despite his many gun battles with the law, he never killed a man. Bill Miner lived through many phases in the development of the American West, including the turbulent post-Civil War era, the last of the stagecoaches, and the change to railroads as the principle means of transportation.

At thirty-three, after his release from San Quentin prison, Miner headed for New Mexico. He worked the fall roundup then moved to Denver. In 1880, Denver was growing fast. Miner adapted to its way of life and was popular with his fiddle in its many saloons. He was handsome and a big hit with the ladies.

As Bill Miner's funds ran low, however, he came in contact with Billy LeRoy. LeRoy is said to be the original Billy the Kid and had a record of stage holdups. The two outlaws formulated plans to rob the Del Norte stage in the San Luis Valley. The stage ran from Del Norte, passed Wagon Wheel Gap, and continued on through Creede and over Spring Creek Pass. It dropped down from the pass then climbed over Slumgullion Pass to Lake City.

Miner and LeRoy "cased" the route for a couple of days. On a December evening they faced the oncoming stage with drawn guns. Miner spoke his classical words, "Hands up." A great deal of gold in the form of dust and coins was removed before the ever-courteous Miner bid the passengers a good evening. Soon a posse was hot on their trail but quickly lost track of the men and gave up the chase. Miner kept the loot and split up with LeRoy.

After some time had passed, Billy LeRoy teamed up with his brother Sam, alias Sam Pond. After two unsuccessful attempts to rob the Del Norte stage, the brothers were captured. They were convicted on May 19, 1881. At midnight that same day, an angry mob pulled them from their cell and lynched them.

After a brief stay in Michigan, Bill Miner returned to Denver. In February 1881, he teamed up with Stanton T. Jones. The two set out to rob none other than the Del Norte stage. Near South Fork, they stopped the stage but got only a few hundred dollars for their efforts. Soon Sheriff Lew Armstrong of Rio Grande County was on their trail. The two outlaws eluded the posse by riding over Marshall Pass and across the San Luis Valley toward Villa Grove.

Armstrong's posse eventually found and captured them, however. Although tied up, the resourceful Miner managed to conceal a revolver. During the night, Miner used his weapon to force the guard to free them. The two outlaws collected their weapons and escaped into the night. The following morning,

Armstrong and his men were able to track the pair. As the posse gained on the outlaws, Miner shot and broke Armstrong's right arm, disabled a deputy's left arm, and winged yet another law officer. Due to his expert marksmanship, Miner escaped to Arizona. As far as is known, he never caused Colorado any more trouble.[6]

Durango's resident outlaw, Ike Stockton, had the sympathy of many citizens until he betrayed Bert Wilkinson for a twenty-five hundred dollar reward. Ike Stockton and his brother, Porter, headed a gang of cattle rustlers. Their methods included crossing into New Mexico to find a herd moving north. They would drive off as many cattle as possible and sell them to the military. Porter was eventually killed near Aztec, New Mexico, by a lawman. Ike escalated his raids on New Mexico cattle to the point that the ranchers were obliged to hire gunmen for their own protection.

In April 1881, a posse of cowboys and gunmen from New Mexico rode north into Colorado to Durango to put an end to Ike Stockton's gang. They traded shots from the mesa east of town with Stockton's men during the course of the day. Hundreds of shots were fired with no fatalities.

Stockton decided that more raids into New Mexico were simply unhealthy and turned to robbing stagecoaches. Bert Wilkinson and two other men, all three of whom may have been part of Stockton's gang, got into some hell-raising in Durango, and as a result, the town marshal was shot to death. The three men rode out of town and stayed at a stage station. The agent's wife sent word to Stockton that the men were hiding at her station. When a reward for twenty-five hundred dollars was offered for Bert Wilkinson's arrest, Stockton yielded to temptation. He lured Wilkinson into the Silverton area and turned him over to authorities. Stockton collected his reward money. Meanwhile, Wilkinson was lynched in the Silverton jail.

On September 26, 1881, Sheriff Barney Watson and Deputy Sheriff James Sullivan attempted to take Stockton in, but the outlaw reached for his gun. The law officers cut him down. Stockton died the next morning and was buried in Animas City near Durango.[7]

One of Colorado's biggest train robberies occurred in October 1881, a few miles north of Colorado Springs. A stack of railroad ties was used to bring the train to a halt. Three men were involved, and they threatened to kill the train crew if the crew failed to comply with their wishes. A volley of shots was fired at curious passengers to drive them back into the coaches. After the messenger opened the door to the express car, the bandits blew open the safe. They escaped with $105,000 in cash plus an additional $40,000 in jewelry. Later, two of the robbers were captured near Corinne, Utah, and returned to Colorado, where they were tried and convicted of the robbery. The third robber died of gangrene as a result of a gunshot wound. The loot, which they had buried along the Bear River, apparently was never recovered.[8]

It was up to law officers Roe Allison and Sheriff Bowman to arrest George Howard Stunce, alias George Howard, wanted for rustling and horse theft. The law officers arrived in Ouray on May 4, 1882. They learned that Howard was working at a nearby ranch. They rode out to the ranch, pretending to be a couple of men interested in investing in a sawmill. They knew Howard was dangerous and wanted to take him by surprise. After a conversation with the outlaw, Allison climbed back into his buckboard and put his shotgun across his knees. Howard was not the least bit suspicious and volunteered to go with the men to show them some fine stands of timber. As Howard turned to get on his horse, Allison jumped down from the buckboard and covered him with his shotgun. He ordered Howard to surrender and to raise his hands. The outlaw went for his gun, and Allison fired both barrels into his side. Instead of falling, the badly wounded outlaw tried to escape. Bowman ran around one of the ranch buildings to intercept Howard. He opened fire on the outlaw with his Winchester. His first shot struck Howard in the left shoulder; his second shot hit Howard in the base of the skull, killing him instantly.[9]

On June 23, 1882, Durango citizens were witness to the town's first legal hanging. More than three hundred attended this public ceremony to see the final moments in the life of George N. Woods. Woods was a gunfighter and had killed at least nine men in less than three years. On May 23, in Durango's Pacific

Club saloon, Woods had argued with M. C. Buchanan. Woods shot Buchanan three times, and after his victim fell to the floor, Woods put one more round into the lifeless corpse. Buchanan was unarmed. What saved Woods from a certain lynching was his immediate arrest.[10]

Deputy Sheriff M. B. McGraw was charged by the Trinidad *Daily News* with allowing prisoners to escape from jail. Sworn statements made by George Goodell said that McGraw received money for each escape. McGraw countered with his own editorial in the Trinidad *Democrat* and accused *Daily News* editor Newell of lying about the matter. McGraw later met Newell and slapped him. He then threatened to kill him.

On August 19, 1882, George Goodell armed himself with a shotgun and boldly walked down the streets of Trinidad. McGraw armed himself with a Colt Navy revolver. The two men passed and repassed each other, working up their courage to take action. Goodell traded his shotgun for a revolver and returned to the street. In the meantime, Newell, fearing what McGraw might try to do to him, kept two loaded revolvers on his desk and a Winchester rifle in the corner.

At 8:45 in the morning, near the office of the *Daily News*, Goodell and McGraw faced each other then reached for their guns. Goodell got off the first shot, paralyzing McGraw's pistol arm. McGraw's revolver fell from his hand and dropped on the sidewalk; Goodell snatched the weapon and fired five shots into the wounded man's body. Deputy Sheriff M. B. McGraw died shortly after the shooting. Goodell was considered to have acted in self-defense, and he was released.[11]

In July 1883, James Lynn was robbed of thirty-two dollars and a silver watch by a couple of ruffians. The incident occurred near Maysville on the east side of Monarch Pass. After the robbery, Lynn was shot and left to die. Lynn recovered, however, and later identified his assailants. The criminals were captured and locked in the Maysville jail. During the night they were removed by an angry lynch mob. The pair was taken over to a large tree and hung. Their lifeless bodies were left swinging until the next morning.[12]

The famous John Henry "Doc" Holliday sprang into action in Leadville on August 19, 1884. He shot bartender Billy Allen in the arm after having borrowed five dollars. Down on his luck, Holliday needed money desperately. Allen made the mistake of threatening to harm Doc should his debt not be paid promptly. Doc Holliday was arrested, tried, and acquitted.

Doc Holliday was the son of a prosperous Southern family. He studied dentistry before contractng tuberculosis in 1873 and moving to the West in search of a better climate. During the next fifteen years, he acquired a reputation as a killer. He practiced dentistry on occasion but more frequently engaged in gambling.

In Tombstone, Arizona, he took part in the gunfight at the O.K. Corral with his friend Wyatt Earp. Holiday died in 1887 of alcoholism and tuberculosis and was buried at Glenwood Springs.[13]

While searching through the Curren home for stolen merchandise, Marshal E. R. Murphy was attacked by an indignant Mr. Curren with a club. To add to his problems, Mrs. Curren came after the law officer with a knife. The wise marshal retreated from this Salida home to a point about twenty feet from the building. He fired a warning shot, which ricocheted, striking Mr. Curren in the head and killing him instantly. This incident occurred in the early part of May 1885, and by May 15, the marshal was indicted by a grand jury for manslaughter because his victim was unarmed. He was tried and acquitted.[14]

George Davis and Harry Banta quarreled over a card game in the town of Monarch. Later, Davis was sitting in a restaurant eating dinner when Banta walked in through a rear door. Without warning, Banta fired twice at Davis. One of the rounds struck Davis in the temple. Banta was arrested, and a livery stable was hired to take him to the Salida jail. Before the trip could begin, however, an angry mob placed a rope around Banta's neck and dragged him down the town's main street until he was dead. The date was June 14, 1888.[15]

Jim Clark was Telluride's legendary marshal. He never drank and had no use for women. Before becoming a Telluride lawman, he fought with Quantrell's notorious guerillas on the side of the Confederacy. Clark turned to a life of crime after the end of the Civil War. He arrived in Telluride in 1887 and worked as a laborer. The existing marshal was unable to keep the lawless element under control. Despite his criminal background, Clark offered to clean up the rough element in Telluride and bring back law and order. He acted so efficiently, using only his fists, that he was quickly appointed city marshal. Clark maintained law and order in Telluride but continued his life of crime outside the city limits. As marshal, he knew of large gold shipments and used this information to tip off his outlaw friends. Clark was even paid twenty-two hundred dollars to be conveniently out of town when Tom McCarty, Butch Cassidy, and Mat Warner robbed the San Miguel Bank. He resorted to disguising himself with black whiskers to hold up miners coming into town to have a good time. Clark would then be amused the following morning when the same miner he had help up would come into his office to report the robbery.

Around midnight on August 6, 1895, Jim Clark was walking down Telluride's main street toward his cabin with another man. A shot rang out from the vicinity of one of the town's many saloons. Clark grabbed his chest, walked out into the middle of the street and looked for his assailant. He returned to the sidewalk and collapsed. The bullet had entered Clark's body above the right breast, passed through one of his lungs, and had come out beneath his shoulder blade. Normally, such a wound would not prove fatal, but an artery was severed. Jim Clark bled to death in fifty minutes.[16]

Lew Vaneck squealed on fellow outlaw William Gibson by telling authorities that Gibson was with him during the holdup of a passenger train near Victor. Deputy Marshal William Shea was sent out on August 11, 1895, to arrest William Gibson and his brother Norman. Shea was successful in finding the brothers and disarming them. The brothers were released, but William Gibson continued to hold a grudge against the marshal. One day, he used his brother to keep track of Shea's movements in Victor. When the right time came, Norman started a commotion and was quickly arrested by Marshal Shea. It was around three o'clock in the morning, and as the two men made their way to the Victor jail, William stepped out of the darkness. He demanded the release of his brother. This prompted Shea to draw, and this was just what William was waiting for. He cut down the marshal with his Winchester rifle, and the lawman died a few days later. The Gibson brothers were apprehended near Fairplay and were tried for and convicted of murder.[17]

The game room in Breckenridge's Denver Hotel was a busy place during the summer of 1898. On August 11, everything was going fine and the rattle of chips could be heard as the faro bank, the roulette wheel, the crap table, and the poker games were in full swing. Just about midnight, four masked men entered through a back door. The gang was led by Louis Scott, alias Pug Ryan. The masked men drew their revolvers, and one of them accidentally discharged his weapon into the ceiling. Everyone in the gaming room was lined up and relieved of their valuables. These included, in addition to a few gold watches, a valuable diamond. The money in the gambling hall's bank was scooped up, and the bandits departed.

A one hundred dollar reward for the arrest of the robbers was offered by the man who lost his diamond. The authorities believed that the robbers were hiding in a cabin near Kokomo (below Fremont Pass). Deputies Ernest Conrad and Sumner Whitney entered the cabin and told the men inside that they planned to search them. They found nothing on the men, apologized, and left. As they were walking away, something caused the lawmen to return to the cabin to continue their search.

As Deputy Conrad began looking at one of the beds, Pug Ryan fired twice, killing the law officer. Deputy Whitney was wounded but managed to get off two quick shots as the bandits fled. His shots were effective, each bullet killing a man. Whitney hung on for two months before he too died.

Pug Ryan was captured four years later, tried, and sentenced to life in prison. He died in 1931 and is buried near the state penitentiary in Canon City.[18]

What is most disturbing about early Colorado justice is the lack of due process. Citizens were constantly taking matters into their own hands, often because of frustration with an ineffective judicial system. Sentences of capital punishment were not in style during the late 1800s, and the populace wanted a more certain end to a given criminal than life in prison. There was no lack of dedication, however, on the part of Colorado law officers. The formality of extradition was often ignored in favor of the more direct method of immediately taking the criminal back to the state or county where the crime was committed. For this reason, law officers roamed freely throughout the West, seeking out criminals with little or no regard for boundaries. But it is these very elements that make the study of the American West most interesting.

Notes

1. These stories and many more are presented in Stanley Zamonski and Teddy Keller's *The '59er's.* (Platte 'N Press, 1961). See pp. 25, 55, 87-91.

2. See *From Mace's Hole,* Beulah Historical Society, 1979, pp. 53-55.

3. See Forbes Parkhill's *The Wildest of the West,* (Henry Holt and Co., 1951) pp. 207-213.

4. A standard work on this and many other subjects is Bill O'Neal's *Encyclopedia of Western Gunfighters.* (University of Oklahoma Press, 1979). See p. 146 for this anecdote.

5. Jack Guian covers this incident in "The Timely End of Jim Moon" in the Denver *Post's Empire Magazine,* April 30, 1967. Also see Frank Freeman's "The Meanest So-and-so in Colorado" in *Real West,* September, 1981.

6. For more on Bill Miner see Ed Kirby's article in the *Quarterly of the National Association and Center for Outlaw and Lawman History,* Vol. X, No. 1, summer, 1985, pp. 3, 4, 5, 6, 16, 17. Also refer to Colin Rickard's article "Bill Miner—50 Years a Hold-Up Man," in the English Westerners *Brand Book,* January 1966, Vol. 8, No. 2, pp. 9-12. This article was continued in the next issue of the *Brand Book.*

7. See Philip Rasch's article "Tom Nance—A Dangerous Man" in *Real West,* March, 1979, pp. 25, 49. Also see *Rocky Mountain Boom Town* by Duane Smith (University of New Mexico Press, 1980) pp. 13-16; and "Gunman of Durango" by Fred Johnson in *True West,* May, 1984, pp. 54, 55.

8. See Richard Patterson's *Historical Atlas of the Outlaw West* (Johnson Books, 1985) pp. 35, 190.

9. This story is covered in Sidney Jocknick's book *Early Days on the Western Slope of Colorado,* pp. 250-256 (Carson-Harper, 1913).

10. See Fred Johnson's "The Hanging of George Woods" in *True West,* December, 1985, pp. 20–23.

11. This story is covered in an article in the Denver *Republican,* August 20, 1882, p. 1 in an article titled, "Riddled with Bullets."

12. See *Under the Angel of Shavano* by George Everett and Dr. Wendell Hutchinson (Golden Bell Press, 1963) pp. 407, 408.

13. See Bill O'Neal's *Encyclopedia of Western Gunfighters,* p. 146.

14. See *Under the Angel of Shavano* by George Everett, pp. 409, 410.

15. See *Under the Angel of Shavano* by George Everett, pp. 413, 414.

16. See Wilson Rockwell's *Memoirs of a Lawman,* (Sage Books, 1962) pp. 186–213.

17. This story is covered in Debbie Johnston's "The Ambush of Deputy Marshal William Shea" in *Real West,* September, 1974.

18. This story is covered in Mark Fiester's *Blasted, Beloved Breckenridge* (Pruett Publishing Co., 1973) pp. 201–204. It is based primarily on newspaper accounts.

INDEX

ABOUT THE AUTHOR

Colorado Gunsmoke is Kenneth Jessen's fourth book on Colorado history. His three previous books are *Railroads of Northern Colorado, Thompson Valley Tales,* and *Eccentric Colorado.* He is also the author of more than 200 published articles dealing with Colorado history as well as numerous articles in both U.S. and European journals on developments within the electronics industry.

Ken is an engineer at Hewlett-Packard and has lived in Loveland, Colorado, for twenty years. He and his wife, Sonje, and their three sons, Todd, Chris, and Ben, all enjoy traveling in the western United States.